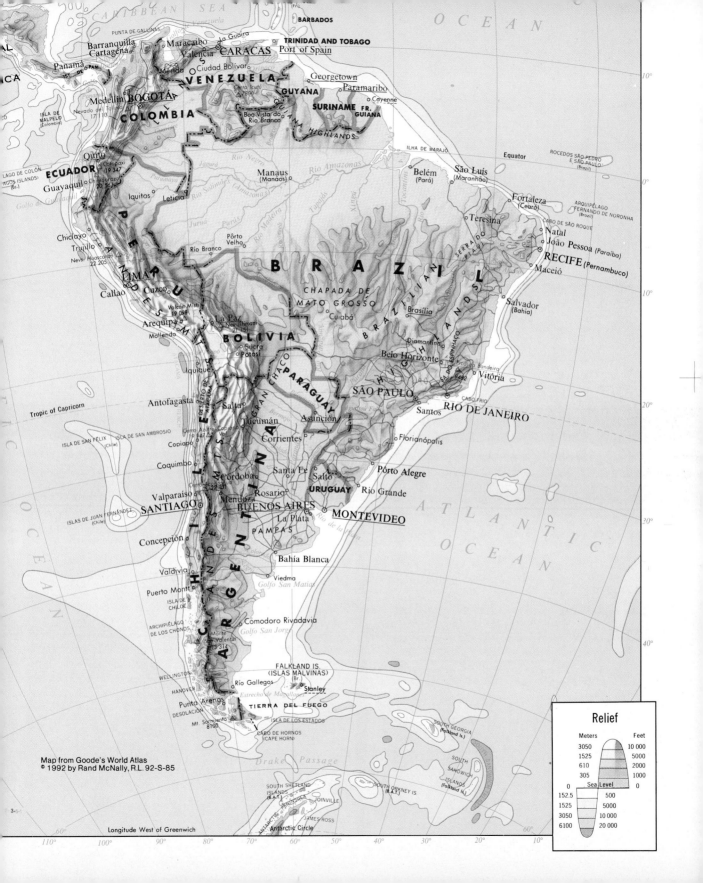

CARIBBEAN SEA

OCEAN

BARBADOS

PUNTA DE GALLINAS
Barranquilla   Maracaibo   La Guaira   TRINIDAD AND TOBAGO
Cartagena   Valencia   CARACAS   Port of Spain
Panamá   Mérida   Ciudad Bolívar
                                                    Georgetown
                 Medellín BOGOTÁ   VENEZUELA   Paramaribo
ISLA DE   COLOMBIA   GUYANA   Cayenne
MALPELO   Boa Vista do   SURINAME FR.
(Colombia)   Rio Branco   GUIANA
                                                         GUIANA HIGHLANDS
                 Quito   ILHA DE MARAJÓ   Equator   ROCEDOS SÃO PEDRO
ECUADOR   Cotopaxi   E SÃO PAULO
LAGO DE COLÓN 19 347   Manaus   Belém   São Luís   (Brazil)
GO ISLANDS   Chimborazo 20 561   (Manáos)   (Pará)   (Maranhão)
(Ec.)   Guayaquil   ARQUIPÉLAGO
                 Iquitos   Leticia   Rio Solimões (Amazonas)   Fortaleza   FERNANDO DE NORONHA
                                                                                        (Ceará)   (Brazil)
Chiclayo   Teresina   CABO DE SÃO ROQUE
Trujillo   Rio Branco   Pôrto   Natal
Nevs. Huascarán   Velho   João Pessoa (Paraíba)
22 205   B R A Z I L   RECIFE (Pernambuco)
LIMA   Maceió
Callao   Cuzco   CHAPADA DE
                                     MATO GROSSO   Brasília   Salvador
Arequipa   Cuiabá   (Bahia)
Volcán Misti
Mollendo 19 098   La Paz   Diamantina
              Nev. Illimani   BOLIVIA   Belo Horizonte
                 21 191   Sucre   Bandeira
Iquique   Potosí   Vitória
                              GRAN CHACO PARAGUAY   CABO FRIO
Antofagasta   Salta   SÃO PAULO
                    Tucumán   Asunción   Santos RIO DE JANEIRO
Copiapó   Corrientes
                                                                  Florianópolis
Coquimbo
              Córdoba   Santa Fe Salto   Pôrto Alegre
Valparaíso   Mendoza Rosario   URUGUAY   Rio Grande
SANTIAGO   BUENOS AIRES   MONTEVIDEO
                    La Plata
Concepción   PAMPAS

Valdivia   Bahía Blanca
Puerto Montt   Viedma   Golfo San Matías
ISLA DE   ARGENTINA
CHILOÉ
ARCHIPIÉLAGO   Comodoro Rivadavia
DE LOS CHONOS   Golfo San Jorge

Tropic of Capricorn   ATLANTIC   20°
ISLA DE SAN FÉLIX   ISLA DE SAN AMBROSIO
(Chile)   (Chile)
ISLAS DE JUAN FERNÁNDEZ
(Chile)   OCEAN

PACIFIC   FALKLAND IS.
OCEAN   (ISLAS MALVINAS)
WELLINGTON   (Br.)
HANOVER   Río Gallegos   Stanley
Punta Arenas   Estrecho de Magallanes
DESOLACIÓN   TIERRA DEL FUEGO
Mt. Sarmiento   ISLA DE LOS ESTADOS
8100   CABO DE HORNOS (CAPE HORN)

Drake Passage   SOUTH GEORGIA
                                                     (Falkland Is.)

SOUTH SHETLAND   SOUTH
ISLANDS   SOUTH ORKNEY IS.   SANDWICH
                           (B.A.T.)   ISLANDS
                                                     (Falkland Is.)
JOINVILLE
ANTARCTIC PENINSULA
JAMES ROSS

Map from Goode's World Atlas
© 1992 by Rand McNally, R.L. 92-S-85

Longitude West of Greenwich   Antarctic Circle

110°   100°   90°   80°   70°   60°   50°   40°   30°   20°   10°

Relief		
Meters		Feet
3050		10 000
1525		5000
610		2000
305		1000
0	Sea Level	0
152.5		500
1525		5000
3050		10 000
6100		20 000

Map from Worldmaster World Atlas
© 1992 by Rand McNally, R.L. 92-S-85

Enchantment of the World

PERU

By Emilie U. Lepthien

Consultant for Peru: George I. Blanksten, Ph.D., Professor of Political Science, Northwestern University, Evanston, Illinois

Consultant for Reading: Robert L. Hillerich, Ph.D., Visiting Professor, University of South Florida; Consultant, Pinellas County Schools, Florida

CHILDRENS PRESS®

CHICAGO

Schoolchildren in Lima

Project Editor: Mary Reidy
Design: Margrit Fiddle

To Marjorie Allen, past international president, the Delta Kappa Gamma Society International

Library of Congress Cataloging-in-Publication Data

Lepthien, Emilie U. (Emilie Utteg)
  Peru / by Emilie U. Lepthien.
    p.   cm. — (Enchantment of the world)
  Includes index.
  Summary: Describes the history, geography, people, economy, and government of the country which lies along the Pacific coast of South America just south of the Equator.
  ISBN 0-516-02610-0
  1. Peru—Juvenile literature. [1. Peru.]
I. Title. II. Series.
F3408.5.L47   1992   92-4813
985—dc20   CIP
                                                     AC

Picture Acknowledgments
AP/Wide World Photos: 62, 63, 64 (right), 65, 67, 68, 69 (2 photos), 70, 72
The Bettmann Archive: 44 (2 photos), 45, 46, 47 (left), 57 (left)
© **Reinhard Brucker: Field Museum, Chicago,** 17 (right), 34 (right), 39 (top & bottom left, top right); **Milwaukee Public Museum,** 21 (left), 22 (top right)
© **Nancy D'Antonio:** 33 (left)
© **Victor Englebert:** 13 (right), 34 (left), 38 (inset), 74 (bottom left), 79, 87 (bottom right), 101 (left), 102 (bottom right), 103 (inset), 106 (bottom left, top right), 113 (inset)

© **Arvind Garg:** 53, 83 (right), 90 (left), 108
© **Virginia R. Grimes:** 40 (bottom left & right)
H. Armstrong Roberts: © **M. Koene,** 102 (left)
Historical Pictures: 31, 42 (left), 56
Emilie Lepthien: 32 (left)
North Wind Picture Archives: 33 (right), 42 (right), 47 (right), 57 (right)
Odyssey/Frerck/Chicago: © **Robert Frerck,** 19, 21 (right), 22 (bottom right), 23 (right), 24, 50 (2 photos), 74 (top right), 90 (right), 101 (top right)
Chip and Rosa Maria de la Cueva Peterson: 4, 74 (bottom right), 76 (2 photos), 80 (right), 91, 93 (left), 94 (right), 105 (right), 106 (top left)
Photri, 105 (left); © **Lance Downing,** 6
© **Carl Purcell:** 12 (left)
Reuters/Bettman: 64 (left), 73, 81, 110 (2 photos), 111
Root Resources: © **Brad Crooks,** 5, 103, © **Ted Mahieu,** 8 (left), 101 (bottom right); © **Shirley Hodge,** 12 (right); © **Steve Carr,** 17 (left), 88; © **Terry Wild Studios,** 74 (top left); © **D.J. Variakojis,** 83 (left), 85, 106 (bottom right), 107 (2 photos)
South American Pictures: © **Robert Francis,** 8 (right); © **Tony Morrison,** 20, 40 (top right), 82 (right), 86, 87 (left), 93 (right), 94 (left), 102 (top right); © **Marion Morrison,** 35, 82 (left)
Tom Stack & Associates: © **M. Timothy O'Keefe,** 29
SuperStock International, Inc.: © **World Photo Service,** 10, 104; © **Kurt Scholz,** 13 (left); © **Steve Vidler,** 14, 26; © **Hubertus Kanus,** 23 (left); © **Augustus Upitis,** 80 (left)
TSW-CLICK/Chicago: © **Michael Scott,** Cover: © **Robert Frerck,** 22 (left), 32 (right), 38, 40 (top left); © **D. E. Cox,** 39 (bottom right); © **Olaf Soot,** 100
Valan: © **Jean-Marie Jro,** 18, 113
Len W. Meents: Maps on 103, 108
Courtesy Flag Research Center, Winchester, Massachusetts 01890: Flag on back cover
Cover: Machu Picchu

Indians in Cuzco pose with their llamas.

TABLE OF CONTENTS

Chapter 1   *Center of the Universe* (An Introduction) 7

Chapter 2   *An Amazing Landscape* (Geography). 11

Chapter 3   *The Pre-Inca Indians of Peru* (Prehistory to A.D. 1000) 16

Chapter 4   *The Mighty Inca* (A.D. 1200 to 1532) 27

Chapter 5   *The Conquistadors and the Colonial Period* (1527 to 1782) 43

Chapter 6   *Independence and the Young Republic* (1790 to the Present) 55

Chapter 7   *Living and Learning* (People, Everyday Life, Education, Religion, Health, Transportation, Communication, Culture, Sports and Recreation) 71

Chapter 8   *Peru's Economy* 89

Chapter 9   *Kingdom of the Sun* (A Tour). 97

Chapter 10   *The Government and Peru's Future* 109

Mini-Facts at a Glance 116

Index 125

Chapter 1

CENTER OF THE UNIVERSE

Peruvians, who have a unique heritage from their pre-Inca and Inca ancestors, feel their country, the Republic of Peru (República del Perú), is very special. The Inca established the capital of their empire at Cuzco, high in the Andes mountains. In the Indian language of Quechua, *Cuzco* means "navel of the universe."

The Republic of Peru lies along the Pacific coast of South America just south of the Equator. The country has rich mineral deposits, yet most of its population is extremely poor. The capital city today is Lima.

THE FIRST INHABITANTS AND THE INCA

Archaeologists believe people have inhabited the coastal plains and mountain valleys of Peru for twelve thousand years. A series of Indian cultures developed during that time. The people were farmers, builders, and artisans. Some tribes in the Amazon region were seminomadic. These diverse ethnic groups were defeated in the fifteenth century A.D. by the Inca, whose military might and administrative ability molded them into a powerful economic and political system. Although the Inca lived in the area around Cuzco

Opposite page: The sacred valley of the Incas, near Cuzco

The Inca farmed on terraces they built on the mountainsides (above) at Cuzco. The ruins of the city of Cajamarquilla (left) are east of Lima.

from about 1200 B.C., they conquered and ruled their vast empire, which included much more than present-day Peru, for less than a century. Weakened by a struggle between two half brothers for the right to be Inca king at the death of their father, the Inca were defeated by Spanish conquistadors under Francisco Pizarro.

Even before the Inca, the Indians had an advanced civilization. For thousands of years the Indians had terraced, irrigated, and raised crops up the mountainsides. The Inca population has been estimated at fifteen million, yet the food supply was abundant. They improved on the agricultural production and kept a three to seven-year food supply in storage.

THE CONQUISTADORS

The *conquistadors* (leaders in the Spanish conquest of Peru) named the high mountain backbone of South America the *Andes,* a name derived from the Indian word for the farming terraces on the mountainsides, *andenes.*

By 1542 the Spanish had consolidated their control over the country and established a viceroyalty. The conquistadors made the Viceroyalty of Peru the richest and most powerful of all of Spain's viceroyalties in America. Lima became the capital.

Peru was the last of Spain's continental colonies to gain independence. Among the country's heroes are Generals Simón Bolívar, José de San Martín, and Antonio José de Sucre. All of these men fought to liberate Peru from Spanish rule. Peru finally declared its independence in 1821.

THE PEOPLE OF TODAY

The Spanish king gave large tracts of land to the conquistadors in appreciation for their service to the crown. The Indians became servants to the Spaniards on what previously had been their own land. Even today the elite of Peru—many of whom are large landowners—are generally the descendants of the Spanish conquistadors and early Spanish colonial officials.

The vast majority of the country's population are Indians, who have little education, own little or no property, and are extremely poor. The gap between the power and wealth of the elite and the poverty of the majority can be compared with the difference between the heights of the Andes and the depths of the valleys.

GREAT ATTRIBUTES

Despite its many problems, Peru is not without great attributes. One of the New World's first universities was founded in Lima.

Zinc and lead mines at Cerro de Pasco

Magnificent churches and public buildings were constructed in the cities of Peru. Outstanding works of art in gold and silver were fashioned by the Inca. Although the conquistadors plundered much of the country's wealth in gold, much still exists to remind the world of the height of Inca civilization. Even roads the Inca and the pre-Inca Indians built can still be found. Fine weaving and pottery from the pre-Inca era attest to the skill of these people. In the desert regions, archaeological remains of vast cities have been found.

Diversified natural resources can contribute to economic development when they are mined. Metallic minerals include gold, silver, copper, lead, zinc, and iron ore. Coal, oil, natural gas, gypsum, phosphate, and other nonmetallic minerals await extraction.

Chapter 2

AN AMAZING
LANDSCAPE

Peru ranks third in size among the countries of South America, with an area of 496,225 square miles (1,285,216 square kilometers). Brazil and Argentina are larger. Peru borders Ecuador and Colombia on the north, Chile on the south, Brazil and Bolivia on the east, and the South Pacific Ocean on the west. It covers an area three times the size of California and is a little larger than the country of South Africa. There are twenty-four departments (political divisions) and one province.

Peru has three major regions: (1) the *costa*, along the Pacific Ocean; (2) the *sierra*, in the Andean highlands; and (3) the *selva* or *la montaña*, which includes the eastern slopes of the Andes and the tropical rain forest of the Amazon River Basin.

THE COSTA

The costa includes the coastal area and the western foothills of the Andes. Although it borders the Pacific Ocean, the barren coastal region of the great Peruvian desert is the driest desert on

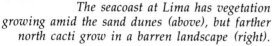

The seacoast at Lima has vegetation growing amid the sand dunes (above), but farther north cacti grow in a barren landscape (right).

earth. Earthquakes occur along the coast, and many of Lima's buildings have been constructed to withstand earthquakes.

The costa has both a high and a low region. Along the costa are twenty-five ports, but there are few good harbors. Sand dunes and dry plains stretch seaward below an altitude of 800 feet (244 meters). Somewhat higher, the Andean foothills are dry and deeply carved by erosion.

Small rivers have made valleys suitable for agriculture, and with irrigation, this otherwise dry region now produces a variety of excellent crops. Most of the farming in the costa is now done by cooperatives, which have replaced the plantations and haciendas that dated back to the Spanish conquest.

THE SIERRA

The sierra, center of the Inca Empire, is a high plateau with three mountain chains in the Andes. It covers a little more than

Chincheros (left), a small town in the Andes, and Lake Titicaca (above), the highest navigable lake in the world

one-fourth of the country's area. The Andes are called the backbone of South America and they extend from the Caribbean Sea at the north end down the entire Pacific Coast of the continent. The Andean ridge has peaks that rise over 18,000 feet (almost 5,500 meters). Here, the Quechua and Aymara Indians still farm the mountainsides, using the terraced fields and ancient irrigation system built centuries ago by their ancestors.

At the Bolivian border is Lake Titicaca, 12,507 feet (3,812 meters) above sea level and 3,200 square miles (8,288 square kilometers) in area. It is the highest navigable lake in the world. The border between Peru and Bolivia divides the lake approximately in half, and the lake is shared by the two countries.

THE SELVA OR LA MONTAÑA

The selva, or la montaña, includes the tropical rain forest and eastern slopes of the Andes. The selva, Peru's largest region, may

An aerial view of the dense vegetation in the Amazon River Basin

be divided into two zones: the low selva, in the Amazon River Basin, and the high selva, or la montaña, which includes the eastern mountain slopes and the valleys. As the snows and glaciers melt, rivers form, flowing swiftly down into the Amazon lowlands.

Few people live in the low selva. Vegetation is dense. The rain forest has few roads, and most travel is limited to the rivers.

The hills and valleys of the high selva link the Andes Mountains with the low selva. The Indians who live near the rivers have agricultural villages; those of the low selva are hunters and gatherers.

The selva yields large quantities of fine timber. In recent years, the discovery of petroleum has brought increased interest in the region.

THE PACIFIC

The Pacific Ocean forms the western boundary of the country. Although there are no large islands, there are about forty small islands off the central part of the coast.

CLIMATE

A cold current flows up from the Antarctic along the coast, called the Humboldt, or Peru, Current. It affects the climate of the costa. Fogs are common and southwest winds blow cold, moist air across the land. In the north where the Andes are farther inland, it seldom rains and the coast is very dry with little vegetation.

On the eastern mountain slopes, however, warm winds carry moisture from the Atlantic Ocean. These winds rise as they reach the mountains. As they cool, they drop their moisture in heavy rains during the Southern Hemisphere's summer, between November and April. Above 15,000 feet (4,572 meters), the precipitation becomes snow.

Several times each decade, great amounts of rain fall along Peru's coast. This severe change in Peruvian weather patterns is called *El Niño*. The name comes from the Spanish *el niño Jesus*, "the Christ child," because it usually begins around Christmastime. During El Niño, warm water from the Equator replaces the cold water of the Peru Current. Heavy rains fall in the coastal desert, and drought occurs in the southern highlands. Drastic flooding has been caused by these storms. Because of the warmth of the water, the fish catch is reduced; birds, who lose their source of food, die and litter the shores. El Niño also affects weather in other parts of the world.

Chapter 3

THE PRE-INCA
INDIANS OF PERU

Long before the Inca dominated the area in South America that includes present-day Peru, Ecuador, Bolivia, Chile, and western Argentina, there were other Indians who had rich cultures of their own. Some anthropologists think people migrated across the Bering Strait on a land bridge between Asia and North America thirty thousand years ago. Some of these people remained in North America; others moved into South America. Perhaps some of the first inhabitants of South America came from the Middle East or the Orient. Some paintings on pottery show people with facial features similar to those of Asians—especially on pottery found in southern Peru. Other anthropologists think that people may have migrated from Polynesia to South America.

EARLY CIVILIZATIONS

Peru has been inhabited for more than twelve thousand years. The first settlers were hunters and gatherers. They hunted wild

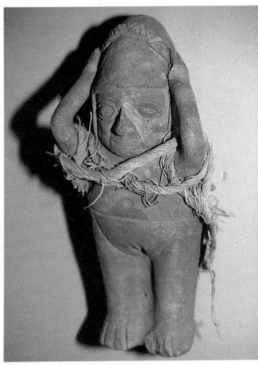

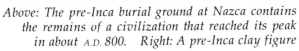

Above: The pre-Inca burial ground at Nazca contains the remains of a civilization that reached its peak in about A.D. 800.   Right: A pre-Inca clay figure

game—llamas, deer, and antelope. Shortly thereafter, they began primitive farming.

The *earliest* Andean inhabitants cultivated various types of beans, fruits, seed plants such as quinoa and amaranth, squash, root crops, potatoes, and corn. Meat from the animals they domesticated or hunted supplemented their diet. The llamas and alpacas provided them with wool and served as beasts of burden. In the valleys between the mountains, these Indians cultivated several varieties of potatoes and corn. The white potatoes we enjoy today were first raised by these early farmers. Small family groups grew into villages and then into very large settlements.

In 1963 explorers discovered Gran Pajaten on the eastern slopes of the Andes in northern Peru. The city was inhabited between A.D. 500 and A.D. 1500. Its multistoried round structures and other buildings made of slate, wood, and a mudlike mortar were discovered in a remarkable state of preservation. Gran Pajaten is not the only pre-Inca city that has been found in the highlands or along the coast in the oases formed by the rivers.

The stonework done by the Chavin people was considered among the finest in the world.

THE CHAVINS

Pre-Inca culture was especially advanced among the Chavins, whose Akaro language evolved into the Aymara language. Aymara is still spoken by a small percentage of the Indian population. The Chavin civilization lasted from about A.D. 200 to A.D. 1000.

The Chavin people were artisans in metalworking. They fashioned the gold jewelry found in the tombs in the north. But their most important contribution to pre-Inca civilization was the cultivation of maize (corn). The large-scale cultivation of maize was carried out on the Andean slopes as far up as 9,000 feet (2,743 meters).

Some of the stones in the Sun Gate weigh up to one hundred pounds (forty-five kilograms).

TIAHUANACO

Near Lake Titicaca about A.D. 800 there arose a great pre-Inca empire, Tiahuanaco, now part of Bolivia. The elaborate tapestries, tunics, and beautiful pottery of these people have been preserved in the desert atmosphere. The capital and ceremonial center built at the southern end of Lake Titicaca was of massive stones held together with notches or inset bronze projections. The Sun Gate, with its sun-god, found its way as a motif into many Andean and coastal cultures. The Indians of Tiahuanaco expanded their empire through conquest and controlled much of southern Peru.

Agricultural terraces were built on the impossibly rocky slopes above the village of Pisac

THE INDIANS OF MOQUEGUA

In southwestern Peru another Andean civilization existed. High above the valley floor, archaeologists have found prehistoric villages constructed on mesas (broad terraces with an abrupt slope on one side) for easy defense. Terraces built on the steep slopes were farmed. Stone-lined canals provided irrigation.

One such terraced city was Cerro Baul above the Río Moquegua. It consisted of twenty acres (eight hectares) of stone houses, two-story buildings, and plazas. Only one steep, narrow path led up to the summit. The inhabitants must have felt their city was impregnable, but later they were conquered by the Inca.

OTHER SOCIETIES

Many other pre-Inca empires and cities developed a high degree of civilization. The Moche and Chicama valleys near the northern coast were linked by canals and an efficient irrigation system. Towns were built on the hillsides above the fields, which were

Mochicas pottery (left) and textile (right)

terraced. Both the terraced fields and town locations maximized the amount of arable land. To increase food production, the Mochicas sailed rafts out to the offshore guano islands, where they collected *guano* (seabird droppings) used to fertilize their fields.

The Mochicas had a highly developed civilization, as evidenced by their housing, clothing, food, and distinctive pottery. They became excellent craftspeople, working with gold, silver, copper, lead, and mercury. They used coal and charcoal as fuels in their furnaces to refine metals. They also created bronze, an alloy of copper and tin. In this way they were able to make tools with sharper blades.

The Mochica people as well as people of other Indian cultures built great ceremonial temples. The largest was the Temple of the Sun in the Moche Valley. The Moche culture existed from A.D. 100 to A.D. 800.

21

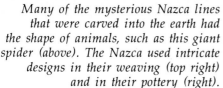

Many of the mysterious Nazca lines that were carved into the earth had the shape of animals, such as this giant spider (above). The Nazca used intricate designs in their weaving (top right) and in their pottery (right).

THE NAZCA AND OTHER GREAT CIVILIZATIONS ALONG THE SOUTHERN COAST

On the south coast another prehistoric culture developed. Between three thousand and four thousand years ago, people who drew enormous designs on the desert floor lived in the valley of the Nazca River. On this Peruvian *pampa* "grassy plain," strange designs are barely visible at ground level but can be seen from the air. No one knows what exact purpose the geometric designs and straight lines served. One theory is that they were used as a calendar.

The Nazca produced great quantities of woven garments: ponchos, shirts, cloaks, and headbands. Intricate designs in weaving, embroideries, and textile painting made the pieces

Remains of the Chimú Empire include walls from their city in Chan-Chan (left) and a drinking vessel of gold and turquoise (right).

distinctive. Nazca pots were also works of art. Molds were used to cast many of their ceramic vessels. Pottery craftspeople worked between 1000 B.C. and A.D. 500.

Along the barren desert coast in northern Peru near Trujillo, the Chimú Empire built its capital city, Chan-Chan. Artisans in Chan-Chan fashioned delicate gold jewelry. They designed silver and gold cups and vases. The Chimú, a militaristic society, built what is now called the Great Wall of Peru. Many feet wide, it began near the coast, extended for many miles across the desert, and ended in the Andes. Forts built along the wall were connected by a wide road 125 miles (201 kilometers) long.

In 1985, still another civilization was discovered in the jungle on the eastern slopes of the Andes. Gran Vilaya, as it is called, covered an area of from 100 to 125 square miles (260 to 324 square

The monastery of Santo Domingo was built over the Inca's Temple of the Sun.

kilometers). The Chachapoya, a warrior group, may have migrated from the Amazon Basin. Only a small portion of their amazing structures has been explored so far. Here, again, the inhabitants built agricultural terraces and farmed.

Pre-Inca civilizations existed in many parts of Peru. When the Inca arrived in Cuzco they built their temples on those of the Indians before them. Later, the Spaniards built on the Inca bases.

FOOD FOR PREHISTORIC INDIANS

River valley plants—peanuts, cucumbers, manioc (from which come tapioca and farina), squash, beans, sweet potatoes, and chili peppers—were a source of food for these pre-Inca Indians of the montaña. There were few animals, but fish and shellfish were abundant in the coastal waters of southern Peru. Coastal dwellers exchanged dried shellfish and salted fish for grains and potatoes cultivated by the Indians in the highlands. As far as thirty-seven miles (sixty kilometers) from the coast, shellfish remains have been found. The Indians of the tropical forest also grew cotton and medicinal plants.

The Indians of the highlands may have followed herds of llamas and guanacos (mammals without humps, related to camels) down to the low hills called *lomas*. The animals searched for grazing areas during the moist coastal winter months. Four thousand years ago, Indian herders built corrals of stone for these animals. Many still stand and are used seasonally by present-day herders.

The early Indian tribes on the coast probably did not use boats for their fishing; however, they did use fishnets that they made of cotton. In the low selva, they also fished with nets or shot the fish with arrows from the riverbanks or from dugout canoes.

Anchovy runs were common, and thousands of anchovies beached themselves on the shore. These anchovy runs afforded the Indians an opportunity to collect fresh fish. They dried the fish for several days, collected the fish oil, and ground the dried fish into meal. The coastal villagers stored the fish meal by heaping it on the ground and covering the heaps with earth to protect them. This preserved the fish meal for several months.

Whale strandings provided the Indians with another source of food. Archaeologists have found whale bones in the refuse of these early cultures. The meat of a beached whale could not be stored, however, so all of the coastal residents came to share in the feast when a beached whale was found and cut up.

A thirty-five-room storage facility has been excavated at El Paraiso. During food shortages, storage facilities had to be defended because other groups would attempt to raid the storehouse.

The pre-Inca Indians of thousands of years ago displayed great ability to draw on their environment for survival. The various tribes spoke different languages and had distinctly advanced cultures, but only the Inca united the tribes under one strong rule.

*Present-day Cuzco, once the capital of the Inca, is about
11,000 feet (3,353 meters) above sea level.*

Chapter 4

THE MIGHTY INCA

An old legend explains the origin of the Inca, the People of the Sun. The sun-god, it is said, created a brother and sister, Manco Capac and Mama Ocllo. They rose out of Lake Titicaca. The sun-god placed the brother and sister on an island in the lake, gave them a gold staff, and told them to wander until the staff sank into the earth, suggesting the fertility of the land.

The sun-god, the legend explains, expected Manco Capac and Mama Ocllo to show humans how to build villages, use the fruits of the earth, and live by the god's wisdom. The sun-god promised to keep humans warm, to grow crops, and to check on the earth each day as he circled the globe.

Scientists and historians know, however, that the Indians present before the Inca knew how to farm, build houses, and to construct and irrigate terraces for their crops. Many of them also worshiped the sun.

CUZCO, CAPITAL OF THE INCA EMPIRE

Manco Capac and Mama Ocllo supposedly wandered northeast over the mountains until they reached present-day Cuzco, perhaps about A.D. 1200, where the staff sank into the ground. About A.D. 1438 Cuzco became the center of the Inca Empire.

INCA ORIGINS

The origins of the Inca are shrouded in mystery. Since they had no written language, they left no record of their accomplishments except as stories, which were told and retold. One legend tells that kinsmen accompanied Manco Capac and Mama Ocllo. Other stories state that Manco Capac, as son of the sun-god, easily became the leader of aborigines living in the region.

CHRONICLERS OF INCA TIMES

Several Spaniards wrote down some of the oral history of the Inca people they encountered. Cristóbal de Molinda, a Spanish priest, wrote *An Account of the Fables and Rites of the Incas* between 1570 and 1584. Garcilasa de la Vega was born in Cuzco in 1540. His mother was an Inca princess and his father a Spanish conquistador who served as governor of Cuzco.

Pedro de Cieza de León arrived in Peru as a Spanish soldier in 1541. He had been fascinated as he watched fabulous gold bars and gold objects being unloaded in Seville in 1534. They were the plunder Pizarro shipped back to Spain when the conquistadors defeated the Inca. Cieza de León spent seventeen years in the land of the Inca. While other soldiers rested, he wrote about the land, the people, and their history. His chronicle is invaluable today.

Cieza de León heard that the Indians living in the mountains worshiped Manco Capac as the son of the sun-god. The natives believed that the Manco Capac of the legend had gained followers and had been able to claim the region and to become the lord of

The annual Inti Raymi sun pageant

Cuzco. Seven of Manco Capac's descendants followed as lords of Cuzco. The sixth lord was the first to use *Inca* as a noble title. The word Inca also was applied to the royal family, descendants of Manco Capac. (Now the word *Inca* refers to all of the people whom they ruled.) The Inca prayed to the sun-god Inti. (Today the Inti Raymi sun pageant is held annually in Cuzco on June 24.)

INCA CONQUESTS AND TAHUANTINSUYU

In the thirteenth century the Inca began their conquest of other nations. Capac Yupanqui, the fifth lord of Cuzco, compelled tribes beyond Cuzco to pay tribute. Tribute was a payment made by tribes and nations to a ruler for peace and protection. Viracocha, the eighth lord, later conquered other tribes and brought them under Inca rule. Historians now believe the people already living in the region had established their own advanced cultures. The Inca were heirs, rather than originators, of the advanced cultures, but they were great organizers.

Tahuantinsuyu was the Inca name for their empire and meant "Kingdom of the Four Quarters." Cuzco was the center of this empire, which was divided into four regions: Chinchasuyu (northwest), Antisuyu (northeast), Collasuyu (southeast), and Contisuyu (southwest). Eventually the Inca Empire extended along the western edge of South America for 2,500 miles (4,023 kilometers), from northern Ecuador east into southern Colombia and south into Chile below present-day Santiago. It included parts of Bolivia and Argentina as well.

A NEW LEADER

About the year 1430, Chanca warriors attacked Cuzco. The Chanca were a powerful nation living west of Cuzco. They believed they were descended from the *puma* (a Quechua word for cougar). The Chanca had encroached on the Inca territory for some time, and they had taken over the Quechua nation in the territory between theirs and the Inca. Viracocha Inca, who had conquered the Indians living around Cuzco, had grown old.

Yupanqui wearing the red-tasseled forehead fringe— the symbol of the Inca king

Viracocha thought the Chanca would be victorious, so he left Cuzco with his son Urcon, whom he had chosen as his successor, for a fortified place away from the city.

But Viracocha's younger son, the Inca prince Yupanqui, battled the Chanca. Using slingshots and rocks that carried farther than the Chanca lances, the Inca defeated their attackers. Yupanqui said that even the rocks turned to warriors. Some of the lords and generals of Cuzco, who had favored Yupanqui over his brother as successor to the king, were so impressed with Yupanqui's courage that they awarded him the red-tasseled forehead fringe, which was the symbol of the Inca king.

The young man chose the name *Pachacuti*, sometimes translated as "He who transforms the earth." Pachacuti was the ninth Inca ruler. He gained so much power that he became the first Inca emperor. It is thought that either his father or his brother tried to kill Pachacuti, but his guards took care of the supposed assassins.

Pachacuti made Cuzco an important ceremonial center. His artisans built walls and structures that stand today. The

Walls built by the Inca are still standing in Cuzco. Stone canals that carried the water for the royal bath still function today (left).

stonecutters split the rocks by drilling small holes in the rock and then using wedges to separate blocks. The stones were so carefully cut and set into place that no mortar was needed, but sometimes they were held together with notches or bronze projections. It is impossible to insert a knife blade between the stones, which were polished with sand and stone. The only tools used were stone hammers, axes, and bronze chisels.

CONQUESTS UNDER PACHACUTI

Pedro de Cieza de León wrote that Pachacuti's armies advanced into the Amazon forests. A second expedition went into Chinchasuyu. In other expeditions Pachacuti's armies captured territory along the Andes from Lake Titicaca to the headwaters of the Marañón River in the north. Eventually, the Inca Empire covered 1.25 million square miles (3.24 million square kilometers) and had a population of more than six million people.

Above: A Peruvian drawing shows Inca warriors with their weapons.
Left: A road constructed by the Inca

ROADS AND HIGHWAYS

All Inca men had to either serve in the army or do public work. Inca warriors used spears, maces, and axes. They were well trained and had excellent leadership. Not only did the Inca have a large standing army, but there were laborers for road and bridge building, the construction of fortifications, and the rock walls of terraces.

Cieza de León wrote that Inca highways were the finest in the world. The network of 10,000 miles (16,093 kilometers) of roads stretched from Colombia to Chile. The coastal road was sunbaked clay. Four stone paved roads radiated from Cuzco, while secondary roads linked the coastal regions with the highlands. Few roads extended into the semitropical forest regions.

Llamas are still used as work animals (left). A diorama shows a typical suspension bridge used by the Inca to cross rivers (right).

The roads were built for travel on foot and for llamas. Rest houses (*tambos*) were built about a day's journey apart. Much later, villages grew up around the tambos. Stone pillars marked distances along the road, much like today's mileage posts. The Inca had no horses. Instead they used llamas. Llamas could not be ridden but could carry heavy loads.

Suspension bridges, the first in the Western Hemisphere, spanned the gorges and rivers. Foot-thick cables were woven of tough fibers from the maguey and aloe plants. The ends of two parallel cables were attached to sturdy stone pillars on the banks. The bridges, used by both men and animals, had handrails and flooring of tightly bound sticks and matting. Highland Indians still build suspension bridges in some remote areas.

COMMUNICATION

Thousands of Inca post runners carried messages from the provinces to Cuzco. A courier system was devised. A runner,

The Inca used quipus, *"knotted strings," to count and keep track of crops, population, llamas, and other data.*

chasqui, ran 2 miles (3.2 kilometers) and then passed the verbal message to the next chasqui. Chasquis also carried *quipus*, "knotted strings," that kept track of the amount of crops, the number of llamas and alpacas, population, birth dates, deaths, and other data. The quipus were passed from runner to runner. Since the Inca had no written language, quipus were very important.

The Inca used the decimal system and zero. In only two other countries was the concept of "zero" or "nothing" used—in India (from which it spread to Arabia and Europe) and in Mexico by the Maya.

INCA GOVERNMENT

The smallest unit of government was the *ayulla*, the village community. Families were grouped into units of ten headed by a leader who assigned work, kept records, and made sure that the people had sufficient clothing, food, seeds, tools, and other necessities.

Each month the leader reported to a chief who headed a group of ten units. When the census was taken, the people in a community were counted in groups of ten (*chungas*), one hundred (*pachacas*), and one thousand (*guarangas*). The census, too, was recorded on quipus. Unfortunately, Spanish conquistadors destroyed Inca storehouses of these detailed accounts knotted onto quipus, and those that have been found cannot be thoroughly understood today. The accuracy of information about distant places and people available to Inca rulers astounded the Spanish.

THE INCA ECONOMIC SYSTEM

Under Inca rule, the land belonged to the empire, whereas families owned their houses and personal belongings. Land was divided into portions. One portion was for the sun and the temple. The second portion was farmed for the aged, ill, widows, orphans, and soldiers on active duty. The third portion was for the family, and a fourth was for the king and government. The chief in each ayulla distributed the land according to each family's needs. The Inca had no monetary system, so the people gave a portion of their produce as tribute to the sun and the Inca ruler.

The Inca rulers wanted their subjects to prosper. Work periods were limited so no one would be overworked. Age limits were placed on workers. People with special skills were employed in stonecutting, metalworking, or other crafts. Everyone was supplied with raw materials, food, clothing, and other necessities. Surplus crops were stored in state and local storehouses to be used in time of war or natural disasters. Wool from llamas and cotton were kept in public storehouses and distributed to the women for spinning and weaving.

SUCCESSFUL EMPIRE BUILDERS

To colonize new territories, the Inca sent their loyal subjects into new regions to explain the Inca system. The abundance of the country was shared by all, and methods of storing surplus crops were employed to prevent famine. To unify their many diverse people and far-flung provinces, the Inca used a common language, Quechua, which they forced conquered nations to adopt. Quechua is still spoken by the Indians of the Andes and by law is one of three official languages in Peru.

Finally, excellent roads ensured a remarkable communication and transportation system.

AGRICULTURE

Three thousand years ago (about 1000 B.C.), in the region around Lake Titicaca, platforms of soil were built around water-filled ditches. Crops were raised despite the altitude and changing weather conditions. The Inca continued to use these same terraced farms and built others. The chief crops grown on these terraces were tubers: potatoes; *oca*, a root herb; and *ulluco*, used in place of potatoes. They are still cultivated today.

Corn and *chuño* were staples in the Indians' diets. Corn, which was grown at lower altitudes, was used fresh, dried, and to make *chicha*, a beer. Corn grows at 8,000 feet (2,438 meters) and in the costa and la montaña. The chuño, freeze-dried potatoes, were processed using the nighttime temperature extreme that occurs in the Andes highlands—there is frost almost every night when the temperature drops. Other foods were also processed for storage in this way; they kept for many years.

At Sacsahuamán are the Inca sun calendar (inset) and the enormous fortress (above) that was begun during the reign of Pachacuti.

The Inca took seeds and roots from conquered nations. They sometimes moved the farmers together with the crops they raised to new regions so that the knowledge of new crop cultivation was assured.

ARTS AND CRAFTS

The clay pottery fashioned by the Inca was not only useful but decorative. Some jars and jugs were shaped in the form of vegetables or humans. Mineral pigments were used to color the pottery in red, black, and white.

The Inca were skilled weavers. Superb textiles and tapestries in a remarkable state of preservation were found in two burial sites in the dry coastal regions. Meticulously embroidered burial robes

Mineral pigments in red, black, and white were used to paint Inca pottery. The same colorful fabric is still woven by the Indians living in Peru.

were uncovered also. Wool, from llamas and alpacas, and cotton were used in weaving. Cotton and wool were traded between coastal and highland people, so the two were often combined in weaving. A shirtlike tunic, *uncu*, and a slit-necked poncho were everyday clothing. The women wore mantles or shawls over their long tunics, fastened with a long silver stickpin, a *topu*.

Straw, cloth, or leather were used in making sandals. Woven belts were wound around the waist.

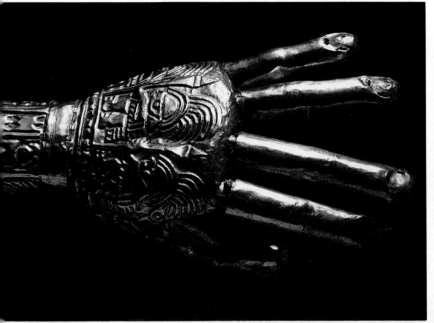

Some of the magnificent pre-Colombian
gold and silver work are (counterclockwise
from above): a golden breastplate,
gold ornaments, a golden hand
used in funerals, and a silver alpaca.

GOLD AND SILVER

Perhaps nothing contributed more to the end of the Inca Empire than gold and silver. To the Inca, gold was the sweat of the sun and silver the tears of the moon.

Most gold came from nuggets and flakes found in the rivers. The precious metal also was mined in the high mountains. The Inca were skilled in smelting, casting, soldering, and making alloys. Bellows and charcoal were used to smelt the gold.

Goldsmiths and much of the golden treasure were brought to Cuzco from the coast. The goldsmiths fashioned cups, religious vessels, necklaces, and even golden hands and arms to cover Inca mummies. Slabs of gold covered the temple walls, and the altars were gold. In a garden, life-size llamas, birds, ears of corn, and other figures, fashioned by skilled goldsmiths, attested to the Inca belief that the sun-god had entrusted them with the safekeeping of gold. Silver deposits were mined in the sierra region. Inca law decreed that all gold and silver belonged to the emperor.

A MIGHTY EMPIRE DESTROYED

There were many reasons why the Inca Empire lasted for scarcely a hundred years after Pachacuti was proclaimed Inca. His reign lasted from 1438 to 1471. His son, *Tupa Inca*, "young king," reigned for the next thirty-two years and expanded the empire south into Argentina and Chile and up the coast to Quito, Ecuador. Pachacuti's grandson, Huayna Capac, expanded the empire east of the Andes and the Marañon and Apurímac rivers up to Ecuador between 1493 and 1527. Huayna Capac was one of the youngest of sixty-two sons fathered by Tupa Inca.

Engravings showing Huáscar (above) and Atahualpa (right)

Huayna Capac died of the plague in about 1527 in Quito. His mummy was returned to Cuzco where Huáscar, the first of his five sons and the one designated to become reigning Inca, was given the imperial red-tasseled forehead fringe.

Huáscar's half brother Atahualpa did not accompany his father's body to Cuzco. When his overtures of friendship to Huáscar were rejected, he proclaimed himself king of Quito, a state separate from the Inca Empire.

Several years later Huáscar sent an inexperienced army against Atahualpa's experienced Inca warriors who had remained in Quito. Huáscar's troops were defeated. Chroniclers reported that 150,000 Indians died in the civil war. Huáscar was executed. In 1532 Atahualpa declared himself the new Inca emperor. The civil war left the Inca Empire weakened and vulnerable to the Spanish invaders.

Chapter 5

THE CONQUISTADORS AND THE COLONIAL PERIOD

THE BEGINNING OF CONQUEST

Francisco Pizarro had accompanied Vasco Núñez de Balboa across the Isthmus of Panama in 1513. While on the Pacific coast he heard stories of a land with long-necked Peruvian sheep (llamas) and hordes of gold. The land lay south along the coast of South America. Balboa, with two new ships, was anxious to sail south. But his rival, the governor of Panama, had Balboa executed before he could sail. Francisco Pizarro took up the challenge, and in 1524 and again in 1526, he set sail for the fabulous land of gold and silver. He reached Colombia on the first expedition and Ecuador on the second. In 1527 or 1528 Pizarro reached Peru and was convinced of its many riches. When he returned to Spain, King Charles I appointed Pizarro governor of Peru.

PIZARRO'S THIRD EXPEDITION

In 1531 Pizarro and his men reached Tumbes, the northernmost coastal village in Peru. He pressed south along the coastal desert

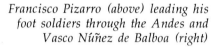
*Francisco Pizarro (above) leading his
foot soldiers through the Andes and
Vasco Núñez de Balboa (right)*

and in November 1532 founded a small settlement in a fertile
valley, San Miguel de Piura. Many years later, after the settlement
had moved to a more healthful site, Piura became a commercial
center for the cotton, sugarcane, rice, and corn grown in the
region.

Using the trails the Inca had built, Pizarro with his foot soldiers,
horsemen, and several guides climbed high into the Andes.
Hernando de Soto, who later found the Mississippi River, and
Pizarro's half brothers accompanied him. They saw results of the
civil war as they moved on toward Cajamarca. They were told
that Atahualpa, the Inca, waited for them there. The climb from
near sea level to the city, at an elevation of 9,000 feet (2,743
meters), was rugged and took more than a week.

On November 15, 1532, the Spaniards looked down on the
valley of Cajamarca. So many tents were seen that at first the
conquistadors must have been fearful. They found the city

This engraving shows Atahualpa being taken prisoner by Pizarro.

evacuated, but Pizarro sent de Soto and fifteen others to meet Atahualpa at a camp four miles (six kilometers) away. A short time later Hernando Pizarro galloped into the camp and informed the Inca emperor that he was the brother of the governor. Atahualpa accepted an invitation to meet the governor, Francisco Pizarro, the next day.

A TRAGIC MEETING

The Inca emperor was carried to the Spanish camp in a golden litter. Singers and dancers preceded him, and his escort remained unarmed, because Atahualpa believed himself to be invincible. But no Spaniards appeared when the Inca and several thousand people filled the plaza. Atahualpa shouted, "Where are they?"

Then a priest stepped forward, demanding that the Inca bow to the church, the pope, and the king. Enraged, Atahualpa refused. He pointed to the sun about to set, and replied, "My God still lives in the heavens and looks down on his children."

Spanish horsemen dashed out from their hiding places. The attack was swift. Accounts differ, but estimates are that from two to seven thousand Indians were slain. The Inca emperor was captured.

Atahualpa's subjects brought precious objects to be used as his ransom.

Atahualpa was treated courteously by Pizarro and encouraged to rule his kingdom while imprisoned. Atahualpa offered to ransom his freedom with a room filled with gold and another room filled twice with silver. Atahualpa sent out a request for gold and silver throughout the empire. Llamas laden with treasure began arriving in Cajamarca.

Impatient, Pizarro dispatched men to Cuzco to loot the Temple of the Sun and to take any other gold they could find. Indians and llamas brought back 285 loads of gold; from another city along the way, 107 loads of gold and 7 of silver were brought to Cajamarca. Beautiful jewelry, ornaments, vessels, and artworks were melted down. There were twenty-four tons (twenty-two metric tons) in all. Each conquistador received forty-five pounds (twenty kilograms) of gold and ninety pounds (forty-one kilograms) of silver.

Pizarro sent his brother Hernando back to Spain with the king's share and sent de Soto to put down a rebellion that didn't exist. Then Pizarro had Atahualpa tried and found guilty of killing

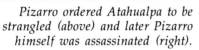
Pizarro ordered Atahualpa to be strangled (above) and later Pizarro himself was assassinated (right).

Huáscar. He was ordered burned at the stake. Atahualpa objected, feeling this would deprive him of an afterlife; he agreed to be baptized instead and took Francisco as his Christian name. Pizarro had him strangled on August 29, 1533.

COMPLETING THE CONQUEST

By November 1533 Pizarro had extended his conquest. In January 1535 Pizarro founded Lima, making it the capital of Peru.

For ten years conflicts between the conquistadors and the Inca warriors continued. In 1537 Diego de Almagro, Pizarro's former partner, tried to take control of Cuzco. In 1538 he was defeated by Pizarro, tried, and executed.

Pizarro extended his power north into Colombia and Ecuador and south into Chile. King Charles I of Spain strongly criticized Francisco Pizarro for executing Atahualpa and for his oppressive rule in Peru. Almagro's followers sought revenge for their leader's execution. In June 1541 they assassinated Pizarro.

ENCOMIENDA

The main reason for Spanish conquest and establishment of colonial empires was to produce revenue for Spain. Gold and silver mining assumed a major role in the economy. Because there was a lenient policy in issuing mining grants, colonists flocked to Peru, which had been named a viceroyalty of Spain. The Spaniards felt it was their legitimate right to enslave the Indians. Under the *encomienda* system, soldiers and colonists were granted land or a village, together with its Indian inhabitants as slaves.

Encomienda gave the colonists both religious and civil authority over the Indians, as well as exacting tribute and labor from them. Through this program, the Spaniards felt they could more quickly convert the Indians to Christianity.

The colonists were anxious to amass personal fortunes. They forced the Indians to transport heavy loads of maize, bars of silver and gold, and other products hundreds of miles across the Andes. Some Indian men were pressed into service as porters for the Spaniards who sought wealth in the Amazon jungle. Others carried artillery across the Andes from Cuzco to Lima, a distance of 400 miles (644 kilometers).

At Potosi, in southern Bolivia, Indian workers from Peru toiled all day in the silver mines. Thousands died. An official sent by the Spanish court reported on the miserable life experienced by the Indians who suffered under harsh conditions, long hours of hard labor, and malnutrition. They had no immunity to diseases brought in by the Spaniards. Thousands died of smallpox and other communicable diseases; those who worked in the mines contracted tuberculosis and other respiratory diseases. Perhaps one-half to three-fourths of the Indian population died.

THE COLONIAL PERIOD

In 1542 the New Laws were written to end the system of encomienda. The colonists, however, felt the Spanish crown was betraying its original covenants of exploration. In 1544 the king sent a viceroy to Peru to enforce the New Laws and to put an end to the rebellious period in colonial conquest.

Peru became an orderly part of the Spanish Empire under Viceroy Francisco de Toledo from 1569 to 1581. Toledo adapted the Indian system of administration to colonial needs. Local chiefs were used as links between the Indians and the Spaniards. The chiefs were to maintain order in their communities, settle minor disputes, and collect tribute. Abuses were curbed, but the Indians still suffered under Toledo.

TRIBUTE TO THE CROWN

One-fifth of the gold and silver sent by way of Panama to Spain was the property of the Spanish crown. Male Indians from age eighteen through fifty-one were required to pay tribute to the crown. Shipments of gunpowder, salt, and tobacco added to Spain's treasury. Dutch, English, and French pirate ships scoured the "Spanish Main" (the Caribbean area), hoping to capture rich prizes of gold and silver on Spanish galleons.

THE ELITE IN THE SOCIAL STRUCTURE

In the Spanish viceroyalty of Peru, life was comfortable for people serving in high administrative positions and for the rich descendants of the conquistadors. Their sons attended schools and

*The Roman Catholic cathedral in Lima (left) used Indian
artists to embellish icons with gold from their temple (right) in Cuzco.*

studied law, theology, and philosophy. The University of San
Marcos was established in Lima in 1551, the first university in the
New World. The clergy, educated in Europe, held a dominant
position in the upper social class.

THE CLERGY'S ROLE

The Roman Catholic church had a strong influence on the social
life of the cities, particularly in Lima. Intellectual and artistic
expression found a welcome in the churches. Indian artists were
set to work embellishing icons with gold that had come from their
own Temple of the Sun in Cuzco. These artists were taught to
copy Old World masters. Some of their religious paintings were
innovative. The Wise Men were depicted riding into Bethlehem on
llamas. Peruvian flowers were banked at the feet of Jesus on the
cross. Their works combined Christian as well as preconquest
religious beliefs.

THE MIDDLE CLASS

Merchants, minor government officials, and skilled artisans lived in more modest surroundings. Most of these people were *mestizos*, persons of mixed race, Spanish and Indian. Many of the minor government officials were Spanish. Some of the artisans were Indian.

These Indian artisans produced objects of wood inlaid with gold. There were frames for paintings in the churches and home altars for the rich. In no other place in the world had such work been done.

Native artists sponsored by Spaniards joined the guilds of the silversmiths and goldsmiths. Before the conquest the Indians had been skilled in producing alloys, soldering, and casting in molds. Under the influence of the Europeans they developed even more complex art forms.

THE INDIANS OF THE POOREST CLASS

The number of Indian artisans was small compared with the rest of the Indian population who were the poorest group. They supplied the manual labor for the mines and the farms. Those living on the fringe of urban centers were often pressed into service as domestic help in wealthy homes or in privately owned textile shops.

The majority lived on large estates or on the sierra hillsides. Often whole families were forced to work for the landowner. Although the law limited the length of service in the mines to a few months at a stretch, many Indians worked for much longer periods.

Some farmed their own small plots on an estate. Because they were rarely paid, they were kept in debt to the landowner for the few necessities they had to buy. There were no opportunities for education, training in skilled occupations, or the chance to move up into the middle class.

THE VICEROYALTIES

Two great viceroyalties had now been established in the New World: Mexico and Peru. Communication between Spain and Peru took as much as eight months on a sailing vessel, so the viceroy was carefully chosen. He had to be capable of making his own decisions; when the colonists became displeased, he had to calm them. It also was his responsibility to see that the Indians were treated fairly. From 1580 until independence in 1821 there was little change in the colonial system.

A PRODUCTIVE SOCIETY

It is difficult to understand how the pre-Incas and the Incas built the terraces and irrigation systems and farmed without iron, wheels, or work animals to pull plows. Yet they produced abundant food for fifteen million or more people. Their storehouses were filled with grains and dried root crops. They could have lived for three to seven years on the abundance they had stored in case of drought, famine, or other natural disasters.

But the conquistadors considered the Inca they defeated to be a backward people. The Spanish replaced many of the native crops with European plants: wheat, barley, carrots, and broad beans.

For almost five hundred years, Indian domesticated plants that

The potato, which might be considered an ordinary vegetable by many people, has a long and noble history.

were high in nutrition, widely adaptable, and very tasty were ignored. But many crops now grown throughout the world originated in the Andes.

The potato, previously unknown outside the Andes, fed the Indians in the silver mines and the sailors on Spanish galleons. After they were introduced in Spain, potatoes spread throughout Europe. Potatoes are now the fourth-most-abundant crop on earth. Tomatoes grew wild in Peru and were about the size of cherries. Large beans were found growing near Lima four hundred years ago. They were called lima beans after the name of the city. They became popular in other countries after growing in Peru for thousands of years.

Chili peppers are one of the most important spice ingredients in the world. The Indians used very hot, pea-sized fruits that had grown on their land for seven thousand years. Originating in the Andes, both wild and domesticated species are still raised locally and also throughout the world.

RIOTS AND REVOLTS

After two centuries of Spanish rule, hard labor and unjust treatment led to riots by the Indians. Local chiefs usually led these revolts. Even the mestizos rebelled against the harsh rule.

Starting in 1780 a series of major rebellions broke out in the highlands of southern Peru and Bolivia. The leader, José Gabriel Cordoncanqui, a mestizo, claimed he was the great, great, great grandson of the last Inca ruler, Tupac Amaru. He chose the name Tupac Amaru II. He and his followers had no clear goals other than fighting in vengeance against Spanish abuses. The uprising spread from Cuzco to Argentina. Outmaneuvered by the Spanish troops, Tupac Amaru II and other principal leaders were captured in 1781. Tupac Amaru II was forced to watch while his wife and sons were executed. He himself then met a gruesome end. The uprising ended in 1782.

CRIOLLO DISCONTENT

The *criollos*, descendants of the Spanish conquerors, were also discontented. Their taxes were high and they had no voice in government. Raw materials were exported to Spain, whereas all manufactured goods had to be imported at high prices.

The criollos resented the European-born Spaniards who enjoyed special privileges. Criollo plans for rebellion were not based on democratic ideals. Instead they sought to build their own industries, manufacture textiles and furniture, and establish their own form of government.

Following the Indian rebellion of 1780 to 1782, the criollos became more aware of their own situation.

Chapter 6

INDEPENDENCE AND THE YOUNG REPUBLIC

A NEW GOVERNMENT

Peru was Spain's strongest power base in the New World. When a new system of administration was applied to all of South America about 1790, the viceroys feared losing their powers. Rumblings of independence surfaced throughout the Spanish colonies.

Napoleon Bonaparte forced King Charles IV and his son Ferdinand VII to abdicate the Spanish throne in 1808. Napoleon appointed his brother Joseph Bonaparte as king of Spain and the Indies.

Some Spaniards seized control of the government and set up military *juntas* "councils" in parts of their country in the name of Ferdinand VII. The juntas established autonomous local governments in the South American viceroyalties. The first revolt against Joseph Bonaparte began in Argentina in 1810 under the leadership of Manuel Belgrano. Belgrano encountered royalist

José de San Martín

troops (troops loyal to the Spanish crown) and a mountain barrier when he attempted to free Upper Peru (present-day Bolivia) in 1813.

SAN MARTÍN LIBERATES PERU

Argentinean-born José de San Martín returned from Europe in 1812 to assist in the revolt against Spain. In 1820 with four thousand troops in his Liberating Army of Peru, San Martín sailed from Santiago, Chile, for Lima. He was successful in routing the royalist army. The royalist governor of Trujillo surrendered his city to San Martín.

On July 14, 1821, the principal citizens of Lima declared Peru independent. On July 28 San Martín issued a formal declaration of independence. At the request of Lima's leading citizens, San Martín took the title "protector," assuming dictatorial powers although he had no desire to hold political office.

Left: The meeting of San Martín and Bolívar in
Guayaquil, Ecuador   Right: The Battle of Ayacucho

THE LIBERATION OF PERU

Venezuelan-born Simón Bolívar had liberated Colombia,
Venezuela, Ecuador, and Panama by 1822. On July 26 and 27,
1822, San Martín met secretly with Bolívar in Guayaquil, Ecuador.
In August 1823, Bolívar sailed for Lima where remnants of San
Martín's forces united with Bolívar's troops to form the United
Army of Liberation. After encounters with royalist troops in the
Andes, Bolívar's army was successful near Ayacucho on December
9, 1824. The Battle of Ayacucho is considered to have ended the
wars of independence not only in Peru but throughout South
America.

The Spanish flag was lowered in Peru on January 23, 1826,
when the last remnants of royalist forces were defeated. Spain did
not formally recognize Peru's independence until 1879.

CONFLICTS IN THE NEW REPUBLIC

Bolívar controlled the country after independence was won. He envisioned a Federation of the Andes composed of present-day Peru, Bolivia, Colombia, Ecuador, Venezuela, and Panama. He was reluctant to permit Upper Peru (Bolivia) to become a new nation, Bolívia.

Caudillos, local warlords, fought each other for control of the country. Several generals also sought control of Peru. In 1827 Marshal José de la Mar, an Ecuadorean, became president.

A conflict with Colombia arose over the territory of Ecuador. For ten years the caudillos fought for control. Finally, an armistice was signed with Colombia. Further problems arose when Ecuador declared its independence from Colombia in 1830.

Bolivian Marshal Andrés Santa Cruz achieved supremacy in Peru after a series of battles and established the Peruvian-Bolivian Confederation, divided into North Peru, South Peru, and Bolivia. In December 1836, Chile declared war against the confederation. Its forces were superior to those under Santa Cruz. Chile won the war in 1839 and the confederation was dissolved. Strife among the caudillos continued for three years. Finally in 1845 General Ramón Castilla assumed the presidency of Peru and ended the supremacy of the caudillos.

A STABLE NATION

The middle years of the nineteenth century have been called the "Age of Castilla." Castilla favored a constitutional republican government. During his sixteen years as president, the country enjoyed social reform and economic development. He worked to settle outstanding foreign debts, bringing the country recognition from other nations.

Rich guano deposits on Peru's offshore islands funded public construction. Guano, composed chiefly of seafowl and bat droppings, is used for fertilizer. The maritime fleet was enlarged. Increased funds were allocated to education and new schools were opened.

The requirement that tribute be paid by all male Indians, dating back to the time of the conquest, was abolished. Slavery was forbidden and Indian rights to communal land were upheld; the civil code was revised.

Freedom of the press was permitted. Literary endeavors in fiction and poetry were encouraged. European immigrants arrived, bringing skills in industry and agriculture. Trade was opened with European countries and with the United States.

CASTILLA'S SUCCESSORS

Many presidents followed Castilla; their time in office was sometimes brief. Hostilities between Spain and Peru erupted when Spain seized several of the guano islands in 1866. A truce was not signed until 1871 and a treaty of peace in 1879.

President Juan Balta, who came into office in 1868, instituted a program of road building and railroad construction to stimulate industry, mining, and agriculture. Manuel Pardo was elected president after the 1872 assassination of Balta.

THE WAR OF THE PACIFIC

Peru feared Chile would annex the rich nitrate deposits in the Atacama desert in the south. In 1873 Peru signed a secret mutual defense treaty with Bolivia, which also held part of the nitrate area and outlets to the Pacific Ocean. This enraged Chile. In 1879 Chile invaded Bolivia, occupying several of its ports. Chile demanded that Peru remain neutral in the dispute. When Peru's attempt to negotiate a peaceful solution failed, Chile declared war. Chile quickly defeated the combined Peruvian-Bolivian forces and also destroyed Peru's navy. In 1881 Chilean forces occupied Lima for two years.

On October 20, 1883, the Treaty of Ancón was signed, putting the disputed region under Chilean control. In 1929 the dispute over the territory was resolved. Chile was awarded the province of Arica and returned the province of Tacna to Peru.

THE STRUGGLE FOR RECOVERY

Peru was bankrupt after the war. The peace treaty had granted Chile half of the revenues from guano for several years, and the nitrate lands had been awarded to Chile. The rail lines built under previous administrations had not resulted in a stimulus to agriculture, industry, and mining.

Financial assistance was desperately needed. Nevertheless, a peaceful period of elected civilian government resulted, and the country restructured its economic system without dependence on the sale of nitrates and guano.

THE TWENTIETH CENTURY

At the beginning of the twentieth century, power remained with the wealthy upper class. But as urbanization and economic development expanded, the middle class grew.

A CHANGING SOCIETY

From 1895 to 1919 a series of civilian governments were elected. Some economic, social, and educational reforms were initiated. Foreign investments were encouraged. Companies from the United States invested in a textile mill, sugar plantations, and refineries. United States businessmen formed the Cerro de Pasco Corporation to mine copper in Pasco Department (state) in the Andes northeast of Lima. The British invested in the International Petroleum Company, later controlled by the Standard Oil Company of New Jersey (Exxon), formed to extract oil from deposits in northwestern Peru. During the regime of President Augusto B. Leguía, the country obtained loans to fund public works and schools.

The American Popular Revolutionary Alliance (APRA) was formed in 1924. This political party advocated equal rights for all citizens—including the Indians—and the nationalization of industries and land.

President Leguía imprisoned his critics, closed the University of San Marcos, and limited freedom of the press. In 1930 he was forced to resign. When APRA launched a rebellion in Trujillo in 1932, the army moved in and shot the rebels. The party continued to gain support, however, throughout the next decade.

ELECTIONS AND COUPS

Throughout the twentieth century the military fostered coups, overthrowing the civilian constitutional government several times.

When Manuel Prado, with APRA's help, was elected president

In 1961 President Manual Prado met in Washington, D.C. with United States President John F. Kennedy.

in 1956 he was faced with serious economic problems and a nearly empty treasury. Drought, earthquakes, and unrest caused by high inflation plagued his administration.

In a military coup days before the 1962 election, Prado was removed from office. The election was canceled. Prado's alliance with APRA and fear that a civil war would result in a disputed election were the reasons given for the coup.

The military junta that ruled Peru for the next year showed respect for personal and political rights and made some attempt at land reform. In 1963 the military supervised a fair and open election.

THE PRESIDENCY OF FERNANDO BELAÚNDE TERRY

Fernando Belaúnde Terry campaigned for the presidency in the 1963 election. He argued that Peru had been conquered by outsiders and it was time for Peruvians to develop their own

*President Fernando
Belaúnde Terry
after his 1963 election*

country. Belaúnde was elected, but his visions of agrarian reform, colonization of the eastern slopes of the Andes by landless Indians from the sierras, and opening the interior were not accomplished.

In 1968 the government agreed to new terms with the International Petroleum Company. Belaúnde's opposition claimed the terms were favorable to the company. Since 1922 there had been controversy over the agreement, and although Belaúnde had promised to settle the controversy within ninety days of taking office, negotiations continued for five years.

Inflation, devaluation of the country's currency, and the suspension of outside economic assistance caused disillusionment with Belaúnde and led to another military coup.

On October 3, 1968, tanks rumbled into the Plaza de Armas facing the Palace of the President in Lima. A group of generals and colonels arrested Belaúnde and drove him to the airport. He was placed on an airplane and flown to exile in Argentina.

A few hours later the commander in chief of the army, Division

Above: The plaza outside the Government Palace after the army overthrew President Fernando Belaúnde Terry in 1968 Left: The Shining Path organization aims to overthrow the government and destroy the economy.

General Juan Velasco Alvarado, assumed the presidency of the Revolutionary Government of the Armed Forces.

THE SHINING PATH

A revolutionary movement called *Sendero Luminoso,* "Shining Path," began at the National University of Huamanga in Ayacucho in 1970. Its founder was Abimael Guzmán Reynoso, a professor at the university. The movement follows Communist ideals. Shining Path wants to overthrow the government and destroy Peru's economy. The movement uses terrorist attacks and assassinations. Security for individuals and businesses has become a necessity.

THE REVOLUTIONARY GOVERNMENT

On taking over in 1968, Velasco Alvarado's government attacked the upper class that had ruled Peru since colonial times.

General Velasco Alvarado became president after the military coup.

It stressed reform of the economic, social, and cultural aspects of Peru. It planned to inaugurate a new nationalistic, independent, and humanistic society that would no longer follow foreign doctrine.

AGRARIAN REFORM

Before 1969, 1 percent of the landowners controlled 80 percent of the arable land. By setting limits on individual land holdings, the government hoped to distribute 72 percent of available arable land to the peasants. The large, profitable coastal sugar plantations were expropriated first; next, the sierra plantations. Although the Agrarian Reform Law of 1969 was one of the most revolutionary and successful land reform programs attempted in South America, the government's goal was never fully accomplished. The lands were not redistributed in individual parcels, but instead were reorganized into cooperatives. The government issued bonds to compensate the landowners.

NEW LAWS AND CHANGING FOREIGN RELATIONS

The government made reforms in education. Programs broadening educational opportunities for Indians and poorer class urban groups were instituted. Adult and vocational education classes were taught in Indian dialects.

Laws governing foreign investments in the fishing and mining industries were changed. Many large foreign companies were nationalized, including the United States-owned Cerro de Pasco copper operation. United States-Peruvian relations were severely damaged when the government took over International Petroleum Company holdings without compensation and United States tuna boats were fired on by Peruvian gunboats.

Breaking what it felt was dependency on the United States, the government developed closer relations with Third World countries.

PROBLEMS ARISE

Finally Velasco Alvarado lost control of his government. The standard of living of average Peruvians had not increased much, and the poor had not benefited as much as anticipated. Miners went on strike. Violent opposition by students and the middle class developed into antigovernment demonstrations. The police went on strike, and riots were frequent between 1971 and 1975. On August 29, 1975, Velasco Alvarado was removed from office.

President Francisco Morales Bermúdez worked to return the government to civilian rule.

Division General Francisco Morales Bermúdez was installed as president. His grandfather had been Peru's president from 1890 to 1894. Morales Bermúdez was more moderate than Velasco Alvarado. He had served as finance minister under Belaúnde and Velasco Alvarado and was respected by both the military and the general public.

Large arms purchases, expensive public buildings, a drop in world prices for sugar and copper, and the failure to develop an expected oil bonanza in the Amazon created severe economic problems. The country was unable to negotiate loans from international banks and the International Monetary Fund.

RETURN TO CIVILIAN RULE

In accordance with the new constitution written in 1979, Morales Bermúdez worked for a return to civilian government.

In 1985 Alan García Pérez became president of Peru.

Elections were held in May 1980. Former President Belaúnde Terry received an impressive plurality that returned him to office.

Once again severe economic problems faced him. Drought in some areas and, from disastrous El Niño storms in 1982 and 1983, floods and a decline in schools of fish in the Pacific created immense financial setbacks.

With high inflation, terrorism, and economic hardship, Belaúnde's popularity declined. The 1983 municipal elections were won by opposition party candidates. APRA candidate Alan García Pérez was elected president in 1985. The transfer of the presidency on July 28, 1985, from Belaúnde to García Pérez was the first exchange between two democratically elected leaders in forty years.

*Above: An area in the Upper Huallaga
Valley that has been cleared for planting
coca bushes.
Left: A farmer harvests coca.*

FOUR YEARS UNDER PRESIDENT GARCÍA

Sixty percent of the world's coca, the source of the drug cocaine,
is grown in the selva in Peru's Upper Huallaga Valley where the
terrorist group Shining Path is active. Farmers find a ready market
for the coca. The United States favored tough law enforcement
and military eradication of drug crops and processing centers.
President García Pérez contended that economic development in
the coca-growing regions would be a better route. He encouraged
the planting of alternative crops.

Following many years of mismanagement, Peru owed
international organizations, foreign governments, and commercial
banks billions of dollars. More than one-third of the debt had

Alberto Fujimori became president in 1990.

been incurred since 1985. García Pérez decided Peru would pay only 10 percent of its export earnings to service its debt. In 1987 the government took over Peru's banks.

THE 1990s: POLITICAL INSTABILITY

At one time García Pérez was so popular there was talk of amending the constitution to allow him to serve a second term. In 1987 he had an approval rate as president of 71 percent. By 1989 it had dropped to 13 percent.

In an election on June 10, 1990, Alberto Fujimori, a university professor of Japanese descent, was elected president. Fujimori was inaugurated on July 28, 1990, but there was concern that he would not carry out reforms to reverse Peru's economic decline.

In 1992 Fujimori suspended the constitution and assumed dictatorial powers, arguing that they were necessary in dealing with the problems of mounting instability, terrorism, and corruption. Disturbed by these developments, the U.S. suspended all aid to Peru in the hope that such a measure might encourage early resumption of constitutional and democratic government in Peru.

Chapter 7

LIVING AND LEARNING

ETHNIC GROUPS

Three principal ethnic groups exist today in Peru: Indians, Hispanicized mestizos, and whites. Blacks and Asians count for about 1 percent of the population.

The whites make up about 10 percent of the population. They are Spanish speaking and well educated. They hold important positions in government, business, and industry and can trace their ancestry to the conquistadors and the first Spanish settlers in Peru.

In the coastal cities, families that have acquired wealth give their children a good education and arrange marriages for them, both of which admit them to elite society. The whites in the sierra, however, have a closed social system. They control local government. The coastal whites control capital and finance.

The Spanish-speaking mestizos make up about 43 percent of the population. They are generally educated. After World War II many became government workers, engineers, administrators in industry, and leaders in reform movements.

The Indians, who make up about 46 percent of Peruvians, are at the lower end of the economic scale. They usually speak only

Children in a town outside Lima wait for trucks to deliver drinking water.

Quechua or Aymara, and their social life is family oriented. Unions, neighborhood associations, and regional clubs are important. Some are skilled or semiskilled workers who migrate from the sierra in search of a better life.

Poor Peruvians often live as urban squatters in shelters of bamboo, mud, and scrap materials. Squatters avoid the high rents frequently charged in urban slums. Squatter settlements, or new towns, as they are called, lack many of the amenities enjoyed by middle- and upper-class citizens. A hillside squatter settlement outside Lima may have a thousand families with only one community water faucet near the bottom of the hill.

THE HACIENDA

The *hacienda*, a large estate or plantation, grew out of the encomienda system. Landholders collected a tax from every male between eighteen and fifty-one years of age. Indians tilled the land for the church and the landholder as they had under the encomienda system.

The poor often live in squatter settlements such as this.

The Indians on the haciendas were assets and were transferred with the land whenever it was sold. Viceroy Toledo tried to establish Indian settlements in which the land was held by the community. These formed the basis of the peasant communities, but haciendas still exist today.

On the haciendas, in exchange for their services, the Indian workers were given a small plot of land, the right to graze a few animals, and sometimes a minimum wage. Women and children often were required to work in the owner's house. A mestizo overseer managed the hacienda for the owner. Many hacienda patrons were fair, but others were cruel, permitting their mestizo overseers to exploit the peasants. Some wealthy hacienda owners still live in Lima and visit their haciendas several times annually.

INDIAN COMMUNITIES

In the hacienda region in the sierra, the status of the ayulla, the Indian community, was often insecure. Hacienda owners often took the ayulla's land. Not until the 1963 constitution was the

*Hats and headdresses are distinctive aspects of some
of the many different Peruvian Indian groups.*

Indian community's right to hold property affirmed. Attempts
were made to establish cooperatives in peasant communities with
some success.

In the tropical forest of the selva, some Indian tribes live near
the rivers in tropical forest agricultural villages. Land is cleared by
the slash-and-burn method. The Indians then plant sweet and
bitter manioc, squash, yams, beans, peanuts, plantains, and maize.
After three or four plantings the yield declines rapidly. Then the
land must lie idle for a time to renew its fertility.

Nomadic tribes live by hunting and gathering. The amount of
wild game has decreased since the introduction of firearms.

With both tribal groups, kinship or the family is the main basis for social organization. Hostilities, however, often exist between different tribes.

EDUCATION UNDER THE SPANISH

Twenty years after Pizarro conquered the Inca, Fray Domingo de Santo Tomas learned the Inca language. He wrote to King Philip saying he found the Inca highly intelligent with a refined language and a high standard of civilization. He wrote a Quechua grammar so other Spaniards could learn the language to use in their daily contacts with the Indians.

After Spanish families arrived in Peru, mothers began giving their children an education at home, while their husbands served in the army or in business. By 1551 private teachers were hired as tutors in reading, writing, and mathematics. Luis de Saavedra, a popular teacher among merchant families, taught not only basic subjects but how to keep account books and write contracts and deeds.

Despite basic knowledge, private education could not award a formal certificate or degree. Several Catholic orders opened tuition-free schools. These schools were open to boys of all social classes. Girls were not admitted. Instead, girls went to convents, where they learned homemaking skills and reading and writing. Religious training was also stressed.

HIGHER EDUCATION

By 1561 Quechua was taught in the cathedral school in Lima, together with the humanities, music, and basic subjects. The

The University of San Marcos, founded in 1551,
has old, as well as modern, buildings.

Jesuits opened the College of San Pablo in Lima in 1568. Students who had completed primary education and wanted to prepare for higher studies in the university enrolled for five years in the college.

Latin was used in most academic books and university lectures, so college students studied Latin. Dramatic programs, poetry competitions, and public debates were part of training at San Pablo.

THE UNIVERSITY OF SAN MARCOS

Dominican friars founded the University of San Marcos in Lima in 1551. It was recognized by Spanish universities and offered degree programs. Fray Domingo de Santo Tomas taught sacred scripture and Quechua using his vocabulary and grammar of the language, which was published in 1560.

Dominican friars held classes in their monastery for twenty

years. In the 1570s Viceroy Toledo decided the university should become a public institution. It moved to a new location near the College of San Pablo in Lima. The university maintains its status as an eminent educational institution and the oldest institution of higher learning in South America.

INDIAN EDUCATION

The conquistadors were intent on converting the Indians to Christianity. Each week they gathered thousands of Indians to teach them Christian doctrine in Quechua.

Primary schools were organized to teach children Christian lessons, Spanish and Quechua, simple arithmetic, music, and sometimes a manual skill or trade. Because many of these schools lacked sufficient funding and trained teachers, they failed. However, in Cuzco and Lima, schools accepted both Spanish and Indian children and provided a good education.

Viceroy Toledo planned special schools for the sons of Inca nobility. The first opened in Lima in 1619 and in Cuzco in 1621. They closed when Peru gained its independence.

THE ARTISANS

Toward the close of the sixteenth century, many European musicians, painters, architects, sculptors, and carvers had arrived in Peru. They worked on building churches, convents, cathedrals, and palaces for the nobility.

Disciples and apprentices gathered in the artists' studios to learn their crafts. They studied under these master craftsmen and artists for several years. Finally they submitted their own work to the board of masters. If their work was deemed a masterpiece, they were accredited and could open their own studios.

Juan de Illescas, a painter, trained members of his own family and other young men in Lima in the 1560s. The Illescas school of painting provided convents and churches with outstanding religious paintings.

Other famous artists included Mateo Perez de Alecio and Angelino Medoro. Alecio trained Pedro Pablo Morón, one of colonial Peru's finest and most prolific artists.

The artisans' guild encouraged teaching and training. As in Europe, there were guilds for silversmiths, blacksmiths, masons, carpenters, tailors, potters, bakers, and candlemakers, as well as for the artists. A few women were guild members. In 1596 Luisa de Rosa became a master potter, Elvira Rodriguez a hatter, and Ana Bautista a master candlemaker.

COLONIAL AUTHORS

The Jesuit José de Acosta arrived in Lima in 1572. Besides being an outstanding teacher and adviser to both the church and state, he also was an author. He wrote about the Indians, their culture, and their abilities and recorded a comprehensive study of the geographical features, flora, and fauna of the country.

Bernabe Cobo mastered both Quechua and Aymara. His great work, *Historia del Nuevo Mundo (History of the New World)* contains information on the geography, plants, animals, and the Indians and their folk medicine. Cobo was one of the first Europeans to describe the quinine tree. He wrote the history of the founding and development of Lima, where he died in 1657.

Among Don Pedro de Perlata y Barnuevo's writings were a

A class in a shantytown school on the outskirts of Lima

study of a comet appearing in Peruvian skies in 1702, histories, religious books, and poetry. He was born in Lima in 1664 and died there in 1743.

EDUCATION TODAY

The present-day law requires all children from six to fifteen years old to attend school. Nevertheless, about one-fourth of all Peruvians fifteen years old or older cannot read or write. Most of these people live in rural areas, or are among the Indian inhabitants of the sierra or the Amazon rain forest. The government has built many rural schools since 1960, but there is still a shortage of both schools and teachers.

Education at the elementary and secondary school levels is free. However, many middle and upper-class students attend private schools where tuition is charged. Public schools are based on class

Above: Students from the Catholic University
Left: The department of education building in Lima

and sociocultural lines. The means for upward mobility depends on attendance in the secondary school and university.

Many men in the armed forces are illiterate and non-Spanish speaking. During their required two-year tour of duty they attend literacy programs.

Some companies have organized training periods to upgrade work skills and have developed apprentice programs. The government sponsors radio and television courses to combat adult illiteracy and to give job training. Public and private universities have been established throughout Peru. There are currently about thirty universities.

RELIGION

Peru's constitution guarantees freedom of religion. About 95 percent of the people are Roman Catholics, but many of the

Contaminated water in this canal near Iquitos is a breeding ground for cholera.

Indian Catholics still worship their Inca gods. The Catholic religion is taught in public schools throughout the country. There are also Protestant, Jewish, and Buddhist groups.

HEALTH

Health care is primarily available in the cities. Almost 59 percent of the hospital beds are in Lima. The rural population has little access to medical services.

In January 1991 an outbreak of cholera added to Peru's health problems. Safe (potable) drinking water is available to about 80 percent of urban residents but to only about 5 percent of those in rural areas. The high infant and childhood death rate is the result of poor sanitation and malnutrition.

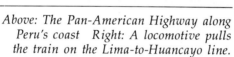

Above: The Pan-American Highway along Peru's coast   Right: A locomotive pulls the train on the Lima-to-Huancayo line.

TRANSPORTATION

The Inca roads built in the Andes are still used, although they are unpaved. The paved Pan-American Highway was built along the Pacific Coast of South America. In Peru it extends 1,710 miles (2,752 kilometers) from the Ecuadorean border to Chile. It connects all of the principal cities and agricultural areas of the costa. A branch extends up to Arequipa.

Of approximately 31,500 miles (50,693 kilometers) of roads, a little more then 10 percent are paved. In the mountains and Amazon basin, roads are inadequate.

There are three main railroad lines. The central system operates from Lima to Huancayo. This line reaches an altitude of 15,844 feet (4,829 meters), higher than any other standard gauge railroad in the world. The Southern Railway runs from Arequipa to Puno and Cuzco. The third railroad runs from Cuzco to Machu Picchu and Quillabamba. Several short-haul lines in the mining region are narrow gauge.

AeroPeru flies tourists to Cuzco (above) and boats (left) are used for transportation on the Amazon and its tributaries.

Callao, near Lima, is Peru's main port on the Pacific. There are six other major ports. Tributaries of the Amazon provide inland waterway transportation. The port of Iquitos at the confluence of the Ucayali and Amazon rivers is the farthest inland deep-water port for ships traveling up the Amazon from the Atlantic Ocean. Several other rivers in the selva are navigable.

Twenty-four airports with paved runways have been built. AeroPeru is the national airline.

COMMUNICATION

El Mercurio Peruano, established in 1791, was one of the first newspapers in South America. Seven newspapers are printed in Lima. Other cities generally have one newspaper.

Today, some television and radio stations are operated by the government, and others are privately owned. Few rural families own television sets but most have transistor radios. Programs are broadcast in Spanish and Quechua.

LITERATURE

Ricardo Palma was Peru's first writer to gain international fame. His works included stories about the time from the Inca Empire to the 1880s.

Cesar Vallejois is Peru's best-known poet. Carlos Herman Belli and Alejandro Romualdo are also contemporary poets. A group of modern poets established the House of Poetry in Iquitos to work together. Cesar Calvo, one of the group's founders, was awarded the National Prize for Poetry in 1972.

Novelists include Ciro Alegria, Carlos Zavaleta, and José Maria Arguedas. The best known of modern writers is Mario Vargas Llosa. In 1982 *The New York Times* named his *Aunt Julia and the Script Writer* one of the twelve best books of the year. He spoke out when the military took over Lima's newspapers in the 1970s. In April 1980 he was a candidate for his nation's presidency.

Sebastian Salazar Bondy, who died in 1964, was the country's most celebrated playwright. Enrique Solari Swayne's *Collacocha* received critical success abroad as well as in Peru.

THE ARTS

In the twentieth century several artists gained international fame. They include Teofilo Castillo, José Sabogal, Julia Codesido, Camilo Blas, and Fernando de Szyszlo. The country's outstanding sculptor is Joaquin Roca Rey.

The National School of Theater Arts and the National Theater Company have encouraged creative activity.

Street musicians playing a harp and flute in Cuzco

MUSIC

The National Symphony Orchestra provides outstanding musical entertainment in Lima. The government supported Conservatory of Music provides training for musicians and composers. Peru's most famous composers include Enrique Iturriag, Celso Garrido Lecca, and Juan Valcarel.

The National School of Folkloric Music and Dance has collected and adapted traditional music from throughout the country.

DANCE COMPETITIONS AND FERIAS

Dancing has played an important role throughout the country. Often it accompanies a *feria,* a town celebration lasting several

The elaborate Inti Raymi festival celebrates the winter solstice.

days. Dance competitions are also popular. Trujillo holds its dance competitions in late January and a spring festival in late September. Puno at Lake Titicaca has the Feast of Calendaria with dancing and music in early February. Arequipa's Festidanza, dance festival, is held in mid-August.

The Inca sun festival is celebrated together with the Feast of Corpus Christi in late June in Cuzco. The Inca held an elaborate celebration, Inti Raymi, at the winter solstice each year. The sun, the ultimate Inca god, was honored in the expectation that it would return to the southern skies again the following year. The festival was banned by the Spaniards, but its revival was proposed in the mid-1940s to coincide with Corpus Christi, a religious feast.

Bullfights and horse racing are two popular spectator sports.

SPORTS AND RECREATION

Soccer is the favorite team sport. In 1969 the national soccer team won a place in the World Cup playoffs. Basketball is also popular. The 1971 South American baseball championship games were held in Lima. Peru sends athletes to the Olympic Games.

Spectators also enjoy bullfights, cockfights, and horse races. Nearby beaches provide young people in Lima with recreation. Only the well-to-do can afford to participate in such sports as golf, tennis, and skiing.

87

Chapter 8

PERU'S ECONOMY

During the nineteenth century Great Britain and France dominated Peru's economy. They were its chief trading partners, investors, and creditors.

In the twentieth century the United States assumed those roles. Following World War II, the United States gave both military assistance and economic aid. Private United States investment increased.

AGRICULTURE

Agriculture provides the income for about 35 percent of the population. Since the Land Reform of 1969, haciendas have given way to cooperatively owned and irrigated farms, located along the coast. They produce cotton, rice, sugarcane, corn, tobacco, chili peppers, grapes, olives, and plum tomatoes for domestic consumption as well as for export.

Only 2.2 percent of the land is arable. Most farmers in the highlands have small subsistence plots where they grow potatoes, corn, beans, grain, and fodder for small herds. Mechanized farming is virtually unknown.

Corn is Peru's most important crop. It is planted in all three regions with the highest productivity in the irrigated costa fields.

Opposite page: Colorful corn and potatoes that have been grown in the mountains near Cuzco

*Harvesting corn (left) and using a traditional Inca digging
stick (right) to prepare the soil for planting*

Corn and potatoes are staples in the Peruvian diet. In particular
regions they are supplemented with cassava, sweet potatoes,
wheat, barley, beans, chili peppers, peanuts, and squash.

Sugarcane was introduced by the Spanish. Its importance as an
export commodity has declined, but it continues to add to Peru's
balance of payments. Coffee, cotton, and sugarcane are the
principal cash crops for export. Cotton is raised primarily in
irrigated fields in the costa. Coffee grows in the sierra and upper
selva.

The need for greater agricultural production and new cash
crops is imperative in Peru. In the early 1980s Peruvian university
researchers studied Andean crops and mountain agricultural
methods. Researchers from Cuzco, Puno, Huancayo, and
Ayacucho participated in fifty projects. Of special interest was the
selection and improvement of quinoa, kiwicha, and kaniwa.

QUINOA

Quinoa was so important to the Incas that it was sacred. In
Quechua it is *chisiya mama*, "mother grain." Each year the Inca

A quinoa harvest

emperor broke the soil with a golden spade and planted the first seed.

Quinoa's protein content is of such high quality that it can take the place of meat in the diet. It sustained Inca armies on their conquests. Its flour can be used for baked goods and other products. Its mild taste is similar to wild rice. Families are encouraged to use quinoa in childhood nutrition programs.

Quinoa is the grain of the future for Peru. Some of the grain is exported to the United States and marketed at gourmet prices. Markets in other countries are sought. Increased production would benefit Peruvian farmers in the sierra highlands by providing an excellent food crop for their families and a cash crop as well. Modern machinery for harvesting and processing quinoa has been developed.

KIWICHA

Kiwicha, a grain, has high levels of protein comparable to those of milk protein (casein). It is colorful, with leaves, stems, and flowers of purple, red, and gold. A single plant can produce 100,000 seeds. Kiwicha is one of the most nutritious foods grown, and is especially good for children, invalids, and the elderly.

The crop is well adapted to the Andes. Forgotten since the Spanish conquest, it is once again being raised as a source of high nutrition as well as a cash crop for Andean farmers. After the grain is threshed, the residue can be used for cattle fodder. During the dry season when forage is limited, the farmer has feed for his small herd.

KANIWA

Kaniwa can be grown in higher altitudes than those sustaining quinoa. For hundreds of years, this nutritious grain fed Indians in one of the world's most unusual agricultural regions. It has a protein content of 16 percent in its cereallike seeds. It may never become an important cash crop but it can sustain families living on subsistence agriculture.

FORESTRY

Most of Peru's forest products come from the lower and upper selva. The cinchona—the source of quinine—grows in the highlands. Of the one thousand varieties of trees in the selva, the most important commercially are mahogany and cedar.

In 1986, the World Wildlife Fund (WWF) backed the Yanesha Forestry Cooperative in the Amazon region in eastern Peru. The Yanesha Indians had permitted logging companies to cut trees in fragile forest land. In 1988 the United States Agency for International Development withdrew from the project because of

The forests of the selva (left) are in danger of extinction.
A sawmill (right) cuts logs from the Amazon rain forest.

Shining Path terrorists in the region. WWF's Tropical Forests
Program increased its financial support. Funds were provided to
the tribe for training, equipment, legal counsel, and technical
assistance.

Now timber harvesting is owned and managed by the Yanesha.
Trees are cut in narrow strips called strip-shelterbelt harvesting.
The strips are cut on a rotational basis and the rest of the forest is
left intact. The timber is shipped down the Amazon River to the
Atlantic Ocean. The tribe derives income from the sale of timber
to local and regional markets and to companies in the United
States and Great Britain.

FISHERIES

Overfishing and El Niño reduced the available schools of fish
some years ago. In 1973 the government nationalized fishing, fish
processing, and marketing. Payments to the former owners and a
reduced catch later necessitated the government sale of the fishing
fleet back to private ownership.

A large anchovy haul (left)
Sacks of fish meal (above) waiting to be loaded onto a ship

Ninety percent of the fish meal made from dried sardines and anchovies is sold throughout the world for livestock feed. Fish oil is also sold abroad.

Fisheries are the country's most important export industry. The catch in 1990 was down from the previous year. In the first half of 1991, export earnings for fresh and frozen fish and other seafood declined due in part to the cholera epidemic.

The controversial 1988 fishing rights agreement with the Soviet Union was revoked in mid-1991 before that country formed a commonwealth of independent states.

MINING AND PETROLEUM

Known deposits of copper, silver, gold, zinc, and iron ore have been mined in the high sierra for many years. Gold and silver were mined by the Inca. There are many mineral deposits in Peru that have not been developed. Copper reserves are sufficient to sustain mining at present levels for another seventy years.

Production of all ores dropped during 1990 through labor unrest, terrorist attacks, lack of financing for improvements, and the country's overvalued exchange rate.

INDUSTRY AND MANUFACTURING

Since World War II Peru has been expanding industrially. Industry is heavily concentrated in the vicinity of Lima and consists mainly of consumer goods. Today large factories produce fish meal, steel, petroleum products, refined sugar, minerals, chemicals, furniture, paper products, cement, processed and canned foods, textiles, and clothing. Many smaller companies and shops, often with as few as five employees, engage in the production of jewelry and art objects.

Unfortunately, private industrial plants and equipment as well as the transportation system and public utilities have lacked the funds to provide maintenance and modernization. Factories often operate at only 50 percent of capacity and many companies have closed.

FOREIGN DEBT

The government has cleared Peru's arrears to the three major international funds. Many companies that were nationalized are being returned to the private sector.

The International Monetary Fund (IMF) once approved Peru's economic stabilization program, but withdrew funding eligibility following on political problems. In 1993 the IMF restored loan eligibility, which will be supplemented when Peru negotiates a feasible debt-reduction program. Peru also owes a large debt to the former Soviet Union and Eastern European creditors. Debt resolution will remain a problem so long as resolution to problems of political instability continue.

TRADE

The United States is Peru's major trading partner, accounting for about 21 percent of Peru's exports. Exports of copper, fish meal, zinc, petroleum, lead, coffee, silver, cotton, and textiles average $3.5 billion annually.

Imports from the United States amount to about $2.3 billion, nearly 28 percent of Peru's total. They include cereals, machinery, chemicals, pharmaceuticals, and petroleum and mining equipment.

Peru also imports products from Japan, the European Community, Brazil, and Andean Pact countries. It exports to Japan, to the European Community, and to other countries.

Before March 1991 most agricultural imports were subject to import quotas. The government eliminated one of the food import marketing companies. A second one continues to operate but without a monopoly on wheat and flour imports. Usually tariffs on varying imports are about 25 or 15 percent. At the end of Garcia's term tariffs were 80 percent.

FOREIGN INVESTMENT

The current government is committed to encouraging foreign investment that is necessary to the economy. Major projects include the Camisea natural gas field and petroleum and mineral explorations. But terrorist activities hinder foreign investment.

Chapter 9

KINGDOM OF THE SUN

Peru is a beautiful, fascinating country. Six of its mountains soar higher than 20,000 feet (6,096 meters) in altitude. The Amazon River, which begins high in the Andes, finally reaches the Atlantic Ocean 3,912 miles (6,296 kilometers) later.

Peru's cities offer visitors contrasts in architecture and style that range from pre-Inca to Spanish conquistador to modern. Peru's art is testimony to the skill of people who have occupied the region for more than two thousand years.

ARCHAEOLOGICAL HERITAGE

Nowhere on the South American continent is there a greater opportunity to study ancient civilization than in Peru. Archaeologists and anthropologists are constantly learning more about Peru's pre-Inca and Inca cultures. Projects sponsored by the National Geographic Society, the Smithsonian Institution, and American and European universities, and Peru's National Institute of Culture are engaged in archaeological excavations. Neither any pre-Inca culture in Peru nor the Inca developed a written language. Only through their art, their buildings, and other archaeological findings are scientists able to study the civilizations that existed before the Spaniards came.

ANCIENT TEMPLE SITES

Ancient temples built between 3000 and 1000 B.C. can be found along the northern coast. A three-thousand-year-old monument center at Cardal is being excavated.

TUCUME

The dry coastal region has preserved the amazing structures built by early inhabitants. Near Peru's border with Ecuador, Thor Heyerdahl, an anthropologist and explorer, has discovered twenty-six large pyramids and many smaller ones in a single temple site at Tucume. The adobe brick pyramids built long ago were eroded by heavy El Niño rains. Irrigation canals show Tucume was an important agrarian center.

THE MOCHE CULTURE—SIPAN

Sipan is south of Tucume on the Pan-American Highway. Apparently the richest treasures were taken by grave robbers, but archaeologists and students unearthed the burial vault of a powerful ancient Mochica leader. He was adorned with gold, turquoise, and lapis lazuli jewelry, the richest find in Peru to date.

PACHACAMAC

Pachacamac in the Lurin Valley is twenty miles (thirty-two kilometers) south of Lima and was once Peru's largest coastal city. The Lima culture (A.D. 1-700) built a small adobe compound. The Ichimay culture (A.D. 1100-1400) built fifteen adobe pyramids.

Excavators found big storerooms yielding corn, chili peppers, and beans. Ceramic and textile workrooms have been opened.

The Sun Temple was erected during the Inca period (A.D. 1440-1533). Solar temples were astronomic observatories. A solar calendar ruled the basic aspects of an agrarian society.

This was one of the cities plundered by Hernando Pizarro in 1533. Ten thousand men carried twenty-seven loads of gold and two thousand pieces of silver from Pachacamac and nearby cities as Atahualpa's ransom.

PARACAS

Farther south is Paracas. In 1925 Julio C. Tello, a Peruvian archaeologist, began a two-year excavation of a mass burial site in Paracas. Mummies buried between 600 B.C. and 150 B.C. were wrapped in finest cotton, alpaca, and vicuna cloth. Skilled weavers produced articles of clothing with elaborate designs and colors. Many textiles were skillfully embroidered.

Tello and his coworkers found dishes of peppers, peanuts, maize, and yucca with the mummies. Ceramics and musical instruments—drums, whistles, rattles, ceramic bells, and reed and pan pipes—probably used in religious ceremonies were discovered also.

LOST CITIES OF THE ANDES

There may be hundreds of "lost" cities on the eastern slopes of the Andes. Located in canyons and jungle areas, they have yet to be discovered. National Aeronautics and Space Administration satellite photographs may locate them.

Spectacular Machu Picchu

MACHU PICCHU

Few archaeological sites are more impressive than Machu Picchu. In 1911 Hiram Bingham, an American scientist, was looking for the last refuge of the Inca. A peasant offered to show him some ruins at the top of a mountain he called *Machu Picchu,* "old peak."

Bingham climbed through a thick jungle and discovered a complex of more than two hundred buildings. Granite stairways, temples, and houses rise 1,600 feet (488 meters) above the Urubamba River. Bingham found objects made of stone, bronze, obsidian, and ceramics but no gold or silver. The Spaniards never found this citadel 70 miles (113 kilometers) from Cuzco.

Why the Inca built the citadel and the reason it was abandoned toward the end of the fifteenth century remain a mystery.

Opposite page: The ruins of Machu Picchu (insets) rise high above the Urubamba River.

Cuzco is at an altitude higher than 2 miles (3.2 kilometers). The market (top right) is always busy with shoppers. Spanish colonial architecture can be seen in the cathedral (left above) and La Compañía Church (inset).

CUZCO

Cuzco, the imperial city of the Inca, is built at an altitude of 11,200 feet (3,414 meters). In this sacred city Inca palaces and temples once stood. Today the triple walls of Sacsahuamán Fortress, the baths of Tampu Machay, the House of the Chosen Women, and granite walls constructed without mortar still stand.

Puno (above and inset) overlooks Lake Titicaca.

Cuzco became a blend of Inca and Western culture when the Spaniards built a magnificent cathedral facing the Plaza de Armas, once the Plaza Huacaypata. Santo Domingo Church was built on the foundations of the Temple of the Sun. Spanish mansions replaced other Inca buildings.

PUNO

Puno overlooks Lake Titicaca and Bolivia. Manco Capac and Mama Ocllo, the Inca's first ancestors, were supposedly created by Father Sun on the Isla del Sol in the lake. Today Quechua and Aymara Indians cultivate potatoes on small plots outside the city; llamas, alpaca, guanaco, and vicuna live on the sierra.

The city of Iquitos on the Amazon River is the home of Peru's Atlantic fleet.

THE AMAZON

The vast rain forest and watershed of the Amazon in the selva cover 60 percent of Peru. There is no road from the costa or the cities in the Andes into the main river port of Iquitos, although the Trans-Andean Highway runs from Lima to Pucallpa. From there a steamer goes to Iquitos and on to the Atlantic. Planes do fly in.

The Amazon and its tributaries provide Peru with a water route from its jungles to the Atlantic. At Iquitos, thousand-ton ships from New York and Liverpool called regularly for rubber from 1880 to 1917. Now the exports include lumber, medicinal plants, orchids, and tropical fish.

TAMBOPATA WILDLIFE PRESERVE

Tambopata Wildlife Preserve has been established by Peru in an almost uninhabited Amazon valley in southeastern Peru. It has the greatest number of exotic plants and animals of any area in the world, and 560 species of birds have been observed.

Above: High-rise buildings in Lima
Right: Police officers in front of the Presidential Palace

AMAZING CITIES TODAY: PERU'S CAPITAL

Lima was founded by Francisco Pizarro on January 6, 1535, along a river the Indians called Rimac. The Spanish thought it was "Limac" and shortened the name to Lima.

The country's government, finance, industry, education, and media are centralized in Lima. Seven million people live in greater Lima, an area of 40 square miles (104 kilometers). Thousands of Andean Indians move to the city searching for a better life. They build *pueblos jovenes* "new towns" of dwellings made from cardboard, tin, and adobe on Lima's hillsides. The suburbs, in contrast, have large homes with patios and gardens.

Around the Plaza de Armas, built by Francisco Pizarro, stand the Presidential Palace, the cathedral with the remains said to be Pizarro's, the city hall, and the Archbishop's Palace. Union Street, a pedestrian mall, connects the Plaza de Armas, with its statue of Pizarro, with the Plaza de San Martín, with its statue of the liberator.

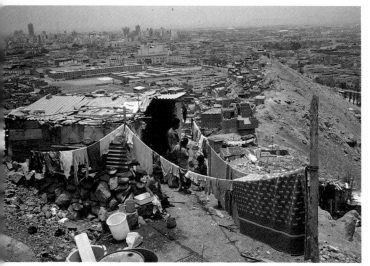
Avenida Benavides in downtown Lima (above) and slums on the edge of the capital city (below).

Street vendors (above) sell everything from magazines to herbal cures. Below: An outdoor café

Lima has many interesting museums. The Museo del Oro (Gold Museum) has more than six thousand gold and silver images, bowls, ceremonial objects, and other items. The Museum of Anthropology and Archaeology exhibits pottery, weavings, and mummies from the ancient cities of Paracas and Nazca.

Spanish colonial churches dominated the city's skyline until fifty years ago. Now modern office and apartment buildings and

El Misti (left) dominates the horizon in Arequipa.   Right: Plaza de Armas

hotels tower above the colonial structures. The modern steel and concrete buildings in Lima, which is in an earthquake belt, have been built to withstand earthquakes.

Callao, nine miles (14.4 kilometers) from Lima, is Peru's main port. Its harbor accommodates ships from around the world. Miles of beaches are located north and south of Lima.

AREQUIPA

Established in 1540, Arequipa is dominated by nearby snowcapped El Misti (19,200 feet; 5,852 meters), a dormant volcano. Diego de Almagro, Pizarro's first partner, was probably the first Spaniard to enter this small town. It was built at the junction of the road from Chile on the south and the road heading north through the coastal kingdoms. Another road led eastward,

A market in Arequipa

ascending the Andean passes to Cuzco. Using this road, runners carried fresh fish from the sea in twenty-four hours to the Inca in Cuzco.

The older houses and churches were built of "sillar," white volcanic stone from the lava of volcanoes around the city. Arequipa, *La Ciudad Blanca* "The White City," gleams in brilliant sunlight.

TRUJILLO

Named for Pizarro's Spanish birthplace, Trujillo was founded in 1532 by Diego de Almagro. In 1537 it was called "Most Noble City of Trujillo" by King Carlos V of Spain. Spanish nobility built magnificent colonial mansions in the city.

The surrounding Moche Valley is a rich agricultural area. Sugar, cotton, rice, and other grains were raised on immense plantations. When agricultural reform in 1969 brought land ownership changes, many plantations became cooperative farms. The region still produces rich crops today.

The colonial mansions, a cathedral, beautiful churches, and the Plaza de Armas in the old city were protected by a wall that was built in 1687 to defend the city from pirates.

Chapter 10

THE GOVERNMENT
AND PERU'S FUTURE

Peru is a democratic republic. Citizens eighteen years of age and over are required to vote. The president is popularly elected for a five-year term and cannot be elected to a second consecutive term. The president appoints a Council of Ministers headed by a prime minister. The legislative branch consists of a 60-member Senate and a 180-member Chamber of Deputies. Congress convenes twice yearly—April 1 to May 31 and again July 27 to December 15. Both congressional bodies can initiate legislation. The president has the power to review legislation. He cannot veto laws passed by Congress. Members of Congress are elected to five-year terms.

All judges in the judicial branch are appointed permanently by the president but must retire at age seventy. The sixteen members of the Supreme Court and the lower court judges are selected from lists given to the president by the National Justice Council.

The nation is divided into twenty-four departments: Amazonas, Ancash, Apurímac, Arequipa, Ayacucho, Cajamarca, Cuzco, Huancavelica, Huánuco, Ica, Junín, La Libertad, Lambayeque, Lima, Loreto, Madre de Dios, Moquegua, Pasco, Piura, Puno, San Martín, Tacna, Tumbes, and Ucayali. There is one constitutional province, Callao. The departments are divided into provinces, which, in turn, are divided into districts.

In attempts to stop the drug traffic, a narcotics officer (left) prepares for the destruction of a coca field in 1990, and in 1989 drugs were confiscated (right) from hidden laboratories and burned.

THE PERUVIAN DRUG WAR

The United States Drug Enforcement Administration works with the Peruvian police and armed forces to eradicate coca plants in the Upper Huallaga Valley in the montaña.

President Fujimori wants to reorganize Peru's economic structure. He thinks if the coca growers had land titles, easy credit, and transportation to bring crops to market, they could be persuaded to grow other crops. At present, attempts to eradicate the coca crop have driven many peasants to the Shining Path.

Latin American leaders maintain that the surest way to destroy drug trafficking would be to eliminate the demand for cocaine in the United States and other countries.

TERRORIST ACTIVITIES

The fighting force of Shining Path numbers between five thousand and six thousand with many more sympathizers

Despite the masks, it is evident that these members of the Shining Path are youngsters.

from the poorer Indian and mixed-race population especially. Shining Path recruits boys from thirteen to fifteen years of age to train as part of its fighting force.

By 1980 the area of Shining Path's influence stretched for a thousand miles along the Andes. It branched into the Amazon jungle and into Lima's shantytowns. Its aims are to wipe out the state and capitalism at any cost and create a worker-peasant state.

During the 1980s and 1990s more than twenty thousand people died at the hands of Shining Path insurgents. They use guerrilla tactics and terrorism. Peru's economic problems under civilian and military rule have provided fertile ground for these guerrillas.

MRTA, the Tupac Amaru Revolutionary Movement, is another Communist terrorist group. Its activities have been concentrated in Lima but are spreading to rural areas. MRTA has participated in bombings, high-profile assassinations, kidnapping-for-profit, and other actions to gain maximum propaganda.

Both Shining Path and MRTA have seriously damaged the country's economy and discouraged investment in Peru, being responsible for more than $15 billion in damage to Peru's economy.

The government declared a state of emergency with decrees to widen military powers to combat terrorism on December 15, 1991. These undemocratic measures caused the United States and others to suspend economic assistance to Peru. However, with government capture of Guzmán, the Shining Path leader, in 1992 and his 1993 sentence to life in prison, government popularity increased. At the same time, there were terrorist attacks and killings in retaliation to Guzmán's conviction. After assuring that Peru would improve its human-rights record, foreign economic assistance programs resumed.

PERU'S FUTURE

President Fujimori inherited serious problems such as soaring unemployment and inflation rates and enormous debts to other countries, banks, and organizations, together with a failing economy. How well he can correct previous mistakes and fulfill his pledge of honesty in government, reduce inflation and renew the economy will restore confidence and reduce terrorist activity. However, there is question of possible government intelligence abuses. President Fujimori's party, *Cambio 90*, "Change 90," is a coalition of people who were excluded from past political activity. But in the 1990 election Fujimori was the only candidate accepted by the middle and lower classes. His plurality was small but the failure of communism should strengthen his party's role.

Peru is a member of the United Nations, Organization of American States, Andean Pact Common Market, Latin American Economic System, Intelsat for International Communications, Non-aligned Movement, African Fund, and the International Monetary Fund.

Peru had a closer relationship with the Soviet Union than any

The Inca trail in the Andes (above)
An Indian spins wool (inset) while her infant sleeps on her lap.

other South American country. It purchased much of its military
equipment from the Soviets. With the end of the Soviet Union in
1991, new alliances with the independent countries in the new
commonwealth will be necessary.

Historically, Peru has had conflicts with Chile and Ecuador.
Currently relations are good. Peru looks to Chile as a model in the
return of democracy and economic development. The president
has expressed his desire to improve his country's observance of
internationally recognized human rights. His goal is to establish a
stable, drug-free, democratic Peru.

MAP KEY

Abancay	D3	Chincheros	D3	Las Piedras (river)	D3, D4	Puno (department)	E3, E
Acari	E3	Chira (river)	B1	Lima	D2	Punta Moreno	C
Acobamba	D3	Chivay	E3	Lima (department)	D2	Puquio	D
Acomayo	D3	Chosica	D2	Lircay	D3	Purús (river)	D
Aguja, Pta. (cape)	C1	Chota	C2	Llata	C2	Reventazón	C
Aija	C2	Chulucanas	C1	Lobos de Tierra, I. (island)	C1	Rioja	C
Alca	E3	Chupaca	D2	Locumba	E3	Rocafuerte	B
Alcoy, Nev. (mountain)	D2	Chuquibamba	E3	Lomas	E3	Salaverry	C
Algodon (river)	B3	Citac. Nev. (mountain)	D2	Loreto (department)	B2, B3, C2, C3	Salcantay, Nevado (mountain)	D
Amazonas (department)	B2, C2	Coles, Punta (cape)	E3	Lurin	D2	San Gallan, I. de (island)	D
Amazonas (river)	B3	Concordia	B3	Machu Picchu (ruins)	D3	San José de los Molinos	D
Ambo	D2	Condor, Cord. Del (mountains)	B2, C2	Madre de Dios (river)	D3, D4	San Martin (department)	C
Ancash (department)	C2, D2	Contamana	C3	Madre de Dios (department)	D3, D4	San Pedro de Lloc	C
Ancón	D2	Contumaza	C2	Mantaro (river)	D3	San Ramón	D
Andahuaylas	D3	Coracora	E3	Manu	D3	Sandia	D
Andamarca	D3	Cordova	D2	Marañón (river)	B2, C2	Santa	C
Andes (mountains)	C2, D2, D3, E3, E4	Coropuna, Nev. (mountain)	E3	Masisea	C3	Santa (river)	C
Andoas	B2	Corrientes (river)	B2	Matarani	E3	Santa Ana	D
Anta	D3	Cotahuasi	D2	Matucana	D2	Santa Clotilde	B
Antabamba	D3	Crucero	D3	Misti, Vol. (volcano)	E3	Santa Isabel de Sihuas	E
Aplao	E3	Curaray (river)	B3	Mollendo	E3	Santiago (river)	B
Apurímac (department)	D3	Cutervo	C2	Monzón	C2	Santiago de Cao	C
Apurímac (river)	D3	Cuzco	D3	Moquegua	E3	Santo Tomas	D
Arequipa	E3	Cuzco (department)	D3	Moquegua (department)	E3	Saposoa	C
Arequipa (department)	E3	Ene (river)	D3	Morococha	D2	Sapuena	B
Ascope	C2	Esperanza	C3	Morona (river)	B2	Satipo	D
Atalaya	D3	Ferreñafe	C2	Morropón	C2	Sayán	D
Atico	E3	Fitzcarrald	D3	Motupe	C2	Sechura	C
Ausangate, Nevado (mountain)	D3	Huacho	D2	Moyohamba	C2	Sechura, Bahia de	C
Ayabaca	B2	Huacrachuco	C2	Napo (river)	B3	Sechura, Desierto de (desert)	C
Ayacucho	D3	Hualgayoc	C2	Naupe	C2	Sicuani	D
Ayacucho (department)	D3	Huallaga (river)	C2	Nauta	B3	Sihaus	C
Ayaviri	D3	Huallanca	C2	Nazca	D3	Sullana	B
Azángaro	D3	Huallay	D2	Negra, Pta. (cape)	C1	Sumbay	E
Azul, Cordillera (mountains)	C2	Huamachuco	C2	Negra, Cord. (mountains)	C2	Suyo	B
Barranca	B2	Huancabamba	C2	Occidental, Cord. (mountains)		Tacna	E
Bayovar	C1	Huancané	E4		D2, D3, E3	Tacna (department)	E3, E4
Blanca, Cord. (mountains)	C2, D2	Huancavelica	D2	Ocoña	E3	Talara	B
Bolivar	C2	Huancavelica (department)	D2, D3	Ocros	D2	Tambo (river)	D3, E
Bolognesi	C3	Huancayo	D2	Olmos	C2	Tambo Grande	B
Borja	B2	Huanta	D3	Omaguas	B3	Tamshiyacu	B
Cabana	C2	Huánuco	D2	Omas	D2	Tantani (mountain)	D
Cabo Blanco (cape)	B1	Huánuco (department)	C2, C3	Orcotuna	D2	Tarapoto	C
Cailloma	E3	Huaral	D2	Otuzco	C2	Tarata	E
Cajabamba	C2	Huariaca	D2	Pacallpa	C3	Tarma	D
Cajacay	D2	Huarmey	D2	Pacasmayo	C2	Tarqui	B
Cajamarca	C2	Huascaran, Nev. (mountain)	C2	Pachacamac (ruins)	D2	Tayabamba	C
Cajamarca (department)	C2	Huaytará	D2	Paita	C1	Tigre (river)	B
Cajatambo	D2	Huaraz	C2	Palpa	D3	Tingo Maria	C
Calca	D3	Ica	D2	Pampas	D3	Toro Rumi (mountain)	D
Callao	D2	Ica (department)	D2, D3	Panao	C2	Titicaca, Lago (lake)	E
Camana	E3	Ilo	E3	Paramonga	D2	Trujillo	C
Campanguiz, Cerros de (mountains)	B2	Intutu	B3	Parinas, Pta. (cape)	B1	Tumbes	B
Cangallo	D3	Iñapari	D4	Pasco (department)	D2, D3	Tumbes (department)	B
Cañete	D2	Iquitos	B3	Pastaza (river)	B2	Tutupaca, Volcan (volcano)	E
Caraveli	E3	Jaén	C2	Pataz	C2	Ucayali (river)	C
Caraz	C2	Jalca Grande	C2	Paucarbamba	D3	Uchiza	C
Carhuaz	C2	Jayanca	C2	Paucartambo (river)	D3	Uinamarca, L. de (lake)	E
Casma	C2	Jeberos	C2	Perene (river)	D3	Urcos	D
Castilla	C1	Juaja	D2	Pevas	B3	Urubamba (river)	D
Castrovirreyna	D2	Juanjui	C2	Pisac (ruins)	D3	Urubamba	C
Catacaos	C1	Juliaca	E3	Pisco	D2	Virú	C
Celendin	C2	Junin, Lago de (lake)	D2	Piura	C1	Vitor	E
Cerro de Pasco	D2	Junin	D2	Piura (department)	B1, B2, C1, C2	Yaco (river)	D
Cerro Azul	D2	Junin (department)	D2, D3	Pomabamba	C2	Yáguas (river)	B
Chachapoyas	C2	La Huaca	B1	Poto (Ananea)	D4	Yanaoca	D
Chala	E3	La Joya	E3	Pozuzo	D2	Yapura	B
Chala, Pta. (cape)	E3	La Oroya	D2	Pucallpa	C3	Yauca	E
Chalhuanca	D3	La Unión	C2	Puerto Bermúdez	D3	Yauli	D
Chan Chan	C2	La Libertad (department)	C2	Puerto Chicama	C2	Yauri	D
Chancay	D2	La Viuda (mountain)	C2	Puerto Eten	C2	Yauyos	D
Chepén	C2	Lachay, Punta (cape)	D2	Puerto Maldonado	D4	Yavari (river)	B
Chiclayo	C2	Lagunas	C2	Puerto Padilla	D3	Yerupajá, (mountain)	D
Chilca	D2	Lamas	C2	Puerto Portillo	C3	Yungay	C
Chilete	C2	Lambayeque	C2	Puerto Supe	D2	Yurimaguas	C
Chimbote	C2	Lambayeque (department)	C1, C2	Puerto Victoria	C3	Zarumilla	B
Chincha Alta	D2	Lampa	E3	Puno	E3	Zorritos	B1

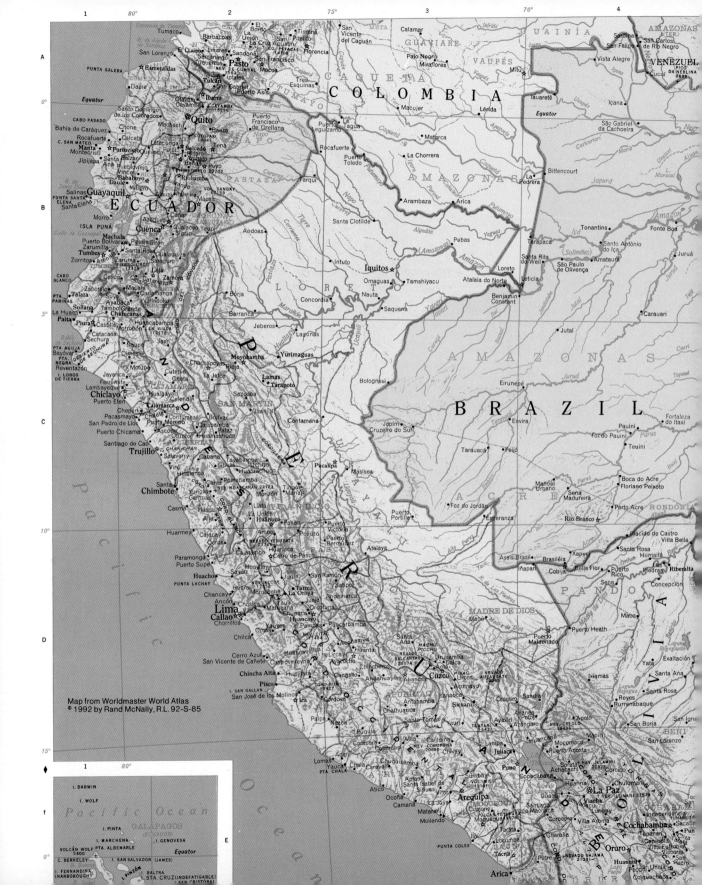

MINI-FACTS AT A GLANCE

GENERAL INFORMATION

Official Name: *República del Perú* (Republic of Peru)

Capital: Lima

Government: Peru is a multiparty democratic republic with two legislative houses, Senate (60 members) and Chamber of Deputies (180 members). Members of the congress and the president are elected for five years. The president, two vice-presidents, and senators are elected in nationwide elections. The president is the head of state and government. Peru's democratically elected former presidents are senators for life. The Supreme Court with 16 members is the highest court of justice. Several layers of courts operate in the judicial system. All citizens over the age of 18 are required to vote in elections.

For administrative purposes Peru is divided into 24 departments and one constitutional province, Callao. The departments are divided into provinces, which in turn are divided into districts.

Religion: Roman Catholicism is the official religion, but freedom of worship is provided for all Peruvians. The Catholic religion is taught in all public schools. About 95 percent of the population follows Roman Catholicism. Some Indian Christians also worship Inca gods. Protestants, Jews, and Buddhists form the other religious groups.

Ethnic Composition: Peru has the largest number of Indians of any country in South America; Indians make up about 80 percent of the population. The Quechua, of pure Indian ancestry, are the largest ethnic group consisting of some 46 percent of the total population; followed by mestizos (people of mixed Indian and Spanish heritage), 43 percent; whites (of European ancestry), 10 percent; and others, 1 percent (mostly blacks and Asians).

Language: Almost 75 percent of the population speaks Spanish. Quechua is the old official Inca language and is spoken by some 30 percent of the population. Aymara is spoken by some 3 percent. All three, Spanish, Quechua (since 1975), and Aymara, are official languages. Many educated Peruvians also speak English.

National Flag: Adopted in 1825, the national flag has three equal vertical stripes, red, white, and red. The national coat of arms is in the center of the white stripe.

National Anthem: *"Himno Nacional,"* beginning *"Somos libres seamoslo siempre"* (We are free; let us remain so forever")

Money: The national currency is the nuevo sol; it is divided into 100 centavos. In 1992 one nuevo sol equaled $ .96 in United States currency.

Weights and Measures: The metric system is in force.

Population: Population in 1993 was 22,889,000; density was 46 persons per sq. mi. (18 persons per sq km). Almost 70 percent of the population lives in urban areas and 30 percent in the rural countryside.

Cities:

Lima	6,404,500
Arequipa	634,500
Callao	588,600
Trujillo	532,000
Chiclayo	426,300
Piura	324,500
Chimbote	296,600

(Population based on 1990 estimates.)

GEOGRAPHY

Coastline: 1,448 mi. (2,330 km)

Highest Point: Mt. Huascarán, 22,205 ft. (6,768 m)

Lowest point: Sea level

Rivers and Lakes: The major rivers, Amazon, Marañón, Huallaga, and Ucayali, all drain east to eventually form the Amazon Basin. Some 50 rivers, starting from the central highlands, flow through the coastal region and provide water for drinking and irrigation. Most of the rivers and lakes are stocked with trout; Lake Titicaca trout average some 22 lbs. (10 kg). Lake Titicaca is the world's highest navigable lake (12,500 ft.; 3,800 m). Peru shares the lake with Bolivia.

Forests: Some half of the land is forests and jungles. Thick rain forests cover the Amazon Basin in the selva. The selva yields large quantities of mahogany, cedar (timber), and cinchona. Overgrazing and soil erosion are a constant threat to the vegetation. Sparse shrub, cactus, and palm grow on the Peruvian coast. Few trees grow on the highlands, but tola and bunch puna grasses grow in abundance on the higher elevations.

Wildlife: Tambopata Wildlife Preserve has been established in the rain forest region of southeastern Peru. It has some 550 species of birds, exotic plants, and wild animals.

Climate: Peru lies very close to the Equator and seasons are opposite to those of the United States. The cold Humboldt Current (called Peru Current) keeps the coastal temperatures fairly cool throughout the year. Temperatures vary more from day to night than seasonally. The snow line is at about 15,000 ft. (4,572 m). Some higher peaks are covered permanently with snow. The rainy season is between October and April. Located on the desertlike coastal area, Lima sometimes does not receive rainfall for many years. Temperatures in Lima are about 55° F. (13° C) in winters and 82° F. (28° C) in summers. The climate is tropical in the eastern region of the Andes. Tropical rain falls almost continuously between October and April. Rainfall increases from the western coast to the eastern selva region.

The warm Pacific current, *El Niño* (the Christ child), comes along the Peruvian coast every few years around Christmas time. El Niño causes serious weather conditions, and has disastrous effects on Peru's fishing industry and the economy.

117

Greatest Distance: North to south, 1,225 mi. (1,971 km)
East to west, 875 mi. (1,408 km)

Area: 496,225 sq. mi. (1,285,216 sq km)

ECONOMY AND INDUSTRY

Agriculture: A little less than half of the population is engaged in agricultural activities, but the yields are low. Most of the farms are very small; some large cooperative farms also exist. Sugarcane, potatoes, rice, corn, sweet potatoes, plantains, cassava, wheat, beans, barley, cotton, and coffee are the chief agricultural crops. Some 400 different varieties of potatoes are grown in Peru. Quinoa, kiwicha, and kaniwa are crops grown since Inca times. Coffee is produced mostly on the highlands.

Peru is the world's leading producer of coca, source of the illicit drug cocaine; some 60 percent of coca is grown in the Upper Huallaga Valley in eastern Peru.

Sheep, cattle, and pigs form the majority of the livestock population. Llama and alpaca hair provide wool for weaving and knitting. Fishing is very important to the economy; Peru's fish catch is among the largest in the world. Fish meal and fish oil are the chief end products. Fish meal is sold throughout the world as livestock feed. Fish catch, largely of anchovettas and sardines, is subject to the disastrous effects of El Niño, as schools of fish die or move far offshore or into deeper waters.

Mining: Peru has some rich and varied mineral resources. The Atacama Desert region in the south holds huge deposits of nitrate, a chemical used to make fertilizers and explosives. Copper, iron ore, gold, mercury, vanadium, zinc, lead, and silver are the chief minerals. Some 40 offshore islands are excellent sources of *guano* (seabird droppings) used for fertilizer. Peru is among the largest producers of silver, copper, zinc, and lead in the world. Petroleum, natural gas, and hydroelectricity are the chief sources of energy production.

Manufacturing: Most of the manufacturing is concentrated along the coastal area, largely around Lima. Cement, animal feed, wheat flour, sugar, sulfuric acid, paper products, chemicals, textiles, furniture, cooking oil, beer, cigarettes, and tires are the chief products. Most of the manufacturing involves processing raw materials for export. Locally knit sweaters with traditional designs, Indian jewelry, and art objects are very popular in the United States and Europe.

Transportation: In the early 1990s there were about 2,140 mi. (3,450 km) of railroads. The central railway extends from Lima to the mineral centers located high in the Andes; this is the highest standard gauge railway in the world. Some roads built by the Incas are still in use. The total road length is about 31,500 mi. (50,693 km), out of which less than 15 percent is paved. The Peruvian section of the Pan-American Highway is paved. Llamas are the beasts of burden in the highlands. In cities most people commute by bus. A very small percentage of the population own automobiles. Lima is the chief international airport; AeroPeru is the national airline. Callao is the major international port on the Pacific. There are six other major ports along the Pacific coast. The Amazon River and its tributaries provide inland waterway transportation.

Communication: Radio and television stations are mostly operated by the government. There are some 70 daily newspapers. Most of the newspapers are privately owned. *El Mercurio Peruano*, established in 1791, was one of the first newspapers in South America. Radio is the chief means of communication. Programs are broadcast both in Spanish and Quechua. In the early 1990s there were 5 persons per radio receiver, 14 persons per television set, and 31 persons per telephone.

Trade: The chief imports are consumer goods, machinery, transport equipment, dairy products, cereals, pharmaceuticals, wheat, and meat. The major import sources are the United States, Germany, Brazil, Argentina, Ecuador, Japan, and Colombia.

The chief exports are copper, fish meal, silver, zinc, textiles, lead, cotton, petroleum and related products, sugar, and coffee. The major export destinations are the United States, Japan, Germany, Venezuela, China, Great Britain, Brazil, and Colombia.

EVERYDAY LIFE

Health: Medical care in Lima is available easily, but rural areas have very few medical facilities. Many Indians are superstitious; they are reluctant to use Western medicine and prefer home remedies. Life expectancy at 61 years for males and 65 years for females is low. Respiratory diseases and infectious and parasitic disease are common. Poor and unsanitary living conditions often are responsible for the quick spread of diseases. A cholera epidemic killed and sickened thousands of people in early 1991. There are about 1,100 persons per physician, and approximately 630 persons per hospital bed in Peru. The infant mortality rate, at 84 per 1,000 live births, is very high.

Education: Education is free and compulsory between the ages of 6 and 15. The government is trying to extend elementary school facilities in remote areas. Secondary education also is free, but there are not many government secondary schools. Private schools are popular among middle and upper-class families. There are some 50 institutions of higher learning, including the University of San Marcos at Lima, which is the oldest in South America. Technical training is provided in some 1,300 vocational and teacher training schools. The literacy rate of the population 15 years and over is 87 percent—one of the highest in Latin America. Adult and bilingual programs and radio and television courses are provided free by the government to combat adult illiteracy.

Holidays:

> New Year's Day, January 1
> Labor Day, May 1
> Day of the Peasant (half day only), June 24
> St. Peter and St. Paul's Day, June 29
> Independence Day, July 28 and 29
> St. Rose of Lima (patroness of Peru), August 30
> Battle of Anzamos, October 8
> All Saints' Day, November 1
> Immaculate Conception, December 8
> Christmas Day, December 25

Movable holidays include Holy Thursday and Good Friday.

Culture: Some of South America's oldest cultures flourished in Peru. Archaeologically important sites include Machu Picchu, Pachacamac, Ollantaytambo, Cuzco, Chan-Chan, and Lake Titicaca islands. Pottery, weaving, woodcarving, silver and golden ware, leather items, and ceramics are the traditional handicrafts still practiced by the Indians. Most of the Peruvian crafts are of Indian origin. Traditional Indian music is played by reed pipes, fiddles, horns, and stringed guitarlike instruments. Plaza de Las Armas in the center of Lima's old section is surrounded by magnificent buildings such as the cathedral and Presidential Palace. The Museo del Oro has a large number of gold and silver images, objects, and other items. The Museum of Anthropology and Archaeology has excellent exhibits from ancient times. Several historically important buildings have been destroyed by earthquakes.

Housing: Most of the whites live in the upper-class fashionable sections of Lima in spacious houses. Large cities also have high-rise apartment buildings. Indian houses in the rain forests region are very small with only a thatch roof; Indian houses in the highlands have thatch roofs and adobe walls. Most of the rural houses have just one room and are built by hand. Crowded and unsanitary shantytowns surround large cities; these houses are made of cardboard, bamboo, mud, old metal, and other scrap material. Only some of these shantytowns, or *pueblos jovenes*, have running water and sewage systems.

Family and Food: The family unit and family ties are very important at every level. Traditional families are large. The father is head of the family and the mother takes responsibility for running the household. Sometimes women work outside the home.

Peruvian meals include soup, rice, beans, fish, potatoes, bread, and tropical fruits. Onions and hot peppers are used for seasoning. Indians of the highlands use corn, beans, and squash as their staple foods. Some Indians chew the leaves of coca to relieve the feelings of cold, hunger, and pain.

Sports and Recreation: Soccer, called *futbol* (football), is Peru's national sport; children as well as adults enjoy this game. Basketball, volleyball, and gymnastics also are popular. Bullfights, cockfights, and horse races are common recreation. Dancing and music are very popular among Peruvians. Golf, tennis, and skiing are sports of the upper class. The National Stadium at Lima is a huge soccer and sports complex. Almost every city celebrates a *feria*, an annual festival to honor its patron saint; fiestas include both Indian and Catholic rites.

Social Welfare: Social insurance is compulsory. Sickness, disability, and old age are covered. The social security system has its own budget. There are also some 100 public welfare agencies.

IMPORTANT DATES

20,000 to 10,000 B.C. — People arrive in South America, almost certainly from Asia

9000 B.C. — Nomadic hunters arrive in Peru

10,000 to 600 B.C. — The Tiahuanaco Empire, first of the Great Andean Empires, extends over the Peruvian coast

900 B.C.—Chavin civilization reaches its peak

850 B.C.—Chavin civilization is well established in the north

A.D. 800—Tiahuanaco Empire flourishes near Lake Titicaca

1200s to mid-1400s—Rise of Inca civilization

1430—Chanca warriors attack Cuzco

1438—Cuzco becomes the center of the Inca Empire

1527—Pizarro reaches Peru; Inca Huayna Capac dies

1532—Spaniards invade Peru under the leadership of Pizarro; towns of San Miguel de Piura and Trujillo are founded

1535—Lima is founded by Francisco Pizarro

1544—Spanish king sends a viceroy to Peru to enforce the New Laws

1551—The University of San Marcos, the New World's first institute of higher learning, is founded at Lima by Dominican missionaries

1560—Santo Tomas's grammar of Quechua language is published

1571—The last uprising of the Incas under Tupac Amaru is crushed

1780—Widespread revolt breaks out against Spanish rule

1781—Uprising is crushed, and Tupac Amaru is executed

1820—José de San Martín invades Peru with an army of Argentines and Chileans

1821—Peru declares independence from Spanish rule

1823—Simón Bolívar, the Liberator, is invited from Venezuela to drive the Spanish out of Peru; General Sucre of Bolivia defeats Spanish forces at Ayacucho

1824—The Battle of Ayacucho is won by Bolívar's army; this ends the wars of independence in South America

1826—Spanish finally surrender in Peru

1827—First constitution goes into effect

1845—Ramón Castilla, of mixed Spanish and Indian heritage, becomes president; he ends the supremacy of the warlords (caudillos)

1864—Spain tries for the last time to gain control of Peru, but fails

1866—Spain seizes several guano islands; hostilities erupt between Spain and Peru

1871—Truce is signed between Peru and Spain over guano islands

1879—Spain formally recognizes Peru; a peace treaty is signed between Spain and Peru over the guano islands; Chile invades Bolivia

1879-83—War of the Pacific; Chile defeats Peru and Bolivia and gains valuable nitrate and silver deposits in the Atacama Desert; Treaty of Ancón is signed

1924—American Popular Revolutionary Alliance (APRA) party is founded

1929—Chile is awarded the province of Arica and returns the nitrate-rich province of Tacna to Peru

1932—APRA launches a rebellion in Trujillo

1948—APRA party is declared outlawed

1955—Peruvian women are given the right to vote for the first time

1956—APRA party is legalized

1963—Explorers discover *Gran Pajaten* city; constitution affirms the Indian community's right to hold property; in a free democratic multiparty election Fernando Belaúnde Terry is elected president

1968—The military overthrows the civilian government and establishes a junta; government agrees to new terms with the International Petroleum Company

1969—Agrarian Reform Laws are passed; the national soccer team wins a place in the World Cup playoffs

1970—Earthquake kills 66,000 people; the *Sendero Luminoso,* "Shining Path"—a Communist terrorist organization—is launched in Ayacucho by Abimael Guzmán Reynoso

1971—Petroleum is discovered for the first time in the northeastern jungle region; South American baseball championship games are held in Lima

1980—A new constitution, written in 1979, is adopted; elections are held; Belaúnde Terry becomes president

1982-1983—Severe economic problems are caused by the return of El Niño

1989—*Cambio 90,* "Change 90," political party is formed by Alberto Fujimori

1990—Presidential elections are held; Alberto Fujimori, a university professor of Japanese descent, is elected president

1991—Cholera strikes some 200,000 people in Peru; cholera-related deaths reach 2,000; a state of emergency is declared to combat terrorism; floods resulting from El Niño damage crops; fishing rights agreement with the former U.S.S.R. is revoked

1992—Shining Path terrorist activities continue; President Fujimori suspends constitution and assumes dictatorial powers; U.S. suspends all aid; Shining Path rebel leader Guzmán is captured

1993—Shining Path leader Abimael Guzmán Reynoso is sentenced to life imprisonment; rebel followers retaliate with terrorist attacks and killings; Peru improves its human-rights record and foreign economic aid resumes

IMPORTANT PEOPLE

José de Acosta (1539-1600), Jesuit missionary, teacher, and adviser; arrived in Lima in 1572

Ciro Alegria (1909-67), novelist; major works are *The Golden Serpent* and *Broad and Alien in the World*

José María Arguedas (1911-69), novelist; major works are *The Deep Rivers* and *Water*

Atahualpa (1500?-33), half brother of Huáscar and son of Huayna Capac; proclaimed himself king of Quito; declared himself Inca Emperor in 1532 after killing Huáscar

Juan Balta (1814-72), president from 1868 until his assassination in 1872

Fernando Belaúnde Terry (1912-   ), founder of Popular Action party; served as president from 1963 to 1968, and again from 1980 to 1985

Carlos Herman Belli, poet

Hiram Bingham (1789-1869), an American scientist; discovered *Machu Picchu* ruins

Camilo Blas, artist

Simón Bolívar (1783-1830), soldier, statesman, and revolutionary leader; known as The Liberator; fought to liberate the country from Spanish rule

César Calvo (1940-   ), poet; one of the founders of the House of Poetry in Iquitos; won the national prize for poetry in 1972

Capac Yupanqui, the fifth lord of Cuzco from 1400 to 1439; compelled Indian tribes to pay tribute

Ramón Castilla (1797-1867), president from 1845 to 1862 with a break of only four years; introduced several economic reforms and developed guano industry

Pedro de Cieza de León (1520-60), Spanish soldier and historian; arrived in Peru in 1541; wrote an account of Inca life and history

Bernabe Cobo (1580-1657), a Spaniard; mastered both Quechua and Aymara; wrote *Historia del Nuevo Mundo*

Javier Pérez de Cuellar (1920-   ), Peruvian diplomat; also Secretary General of the United Nations from 1981 to 1991

Alberto Fujimori (1938-   ), an agronomist of Japanese origin; president since 1990

Alan García Pérez (1949-   ), elected president in 1982

Celso Garrido Lecca, composer of music

Abimael Guzmán Reynoso, (1934-   ), founder of the Communist terrorist organization the Shining Path

Huáscar (1495?-1533), oldest son of Huayna Capac; became Inca after the death of his father

Huayna Capac (1450?-1527), greatest Inca ruler; grandson of Pachacuti; expanded his empire east of the Andes between 1493 and 1527

Alexander von Humboldt (1769-1859), scientist and naturalist

Augusto B. Leguía (1863-1932), president of Peru from 1908 to 1912 and 1919 to 1930; overthrown by military revolt in 1930

Mama Ocllo, daughter of the sun-god; created with brother Manco Capac

Manco Capac, son of the sun-god; created with sister Mama Ocllo

José de la Mar (1788-1839), Ecuadorean; president of Peru in 1827

Francisco Morales Bermúdez (1921-   ), military president during 1975 and 1980; prepared the country for a return to civilian rule

Pachacuti or Yupanqui (-d.1471), the ninth Inca ruler and the first Inca Emperor; reign lasted from 1438 to 1471

Ricardo Palma (1833-1919), Peru's greatest literary figure; wrote about life in colonial Peru; work includes *Tradiciones Peruanas*

Don Pedro de Peralta y Barnuevo (1664-1743), writer, historian, and poet; wrote about a comet appearing in Peruvian skies in 1702

Mateo Pérez de Alecio, artist; teacher of Pedro Pablo Morón

Francisco Pizarro (1475-1541), Spanish conquistador; conquered the Inca Empire in Peru 1531-35; founded Lima in 1535

José Sabogal (1888-1956), artist and painter; started the Indianism movement

Sebastian Salazar Bondy (1924-64), writer and poet; works include *Lima the Horrible* and *Rodil*

José de San Martín (1778-1850), soldier and statesman; Latin American hero who fought against Spanish rule

Fray Domingo de Santo Tomas, Spaniard who learned the Inca language; he also wrote a Quechua grammar

Enrique Solari Swayne (1915-   ), writer and playwright; his *Collacocha* received critical success abroad as well as acclaim in Peru

Antonio José de Sucre (1795-1830), one of Bolívar's generals; president of Bolivia from 1826 to 1828

Victor Raul Haya de la Torre (1895-1979), founder of the American Popular Revolutionary Alliance (APRA) party

Tupa Inca, son of Pachacuti; expanded his empire south into Argentina and Chile; reigned between 1471 and 1493

Tupac Amaru (?-1572), Inca chieftain

Tupac Amaru II (José Gabriel Cordoncanqui) (1742-81), part-Inca; led a revolution against Spanish rule in 1780

Cesar Vallejois (1895-1938), poet; works include *Human Poems*

Mario Vargas Llosa (1936-   ), novelist and politician; unsuccessfully ran for presidential office in 1990; works include *The City and the Dogs, Aunt Julia and the Script Writer,* and *The Green House*

Juan Velasco Alvarado (1910-77), military general; led coup in 1968; ousted in 1975

Viracocha, the eighth lord of Cuzco; brought several tribes under Inca rule

INDEX

Page numbers that appear in boldface type indicate illustrations

Acosta, José de, 78, 123
African Fund, 112
Agency for International Development, 92-93
Agrarian Reform Law (1969), 65-66, 89, 108, 122
air travel, 83, **83**, 118
Akaro language, 18
Alegria, Ciro, 84, 123
Almagro, Diego de, 47, 107, 108
alpacas, 35
Amazon rain forest, 79, **93**
Amazon River, 83, 93, 97, 104, **104**, 117, 118
Amazon River Basin, 11, 14, **14**, 117
Amazonas (department), 109
American Popular Revolutionary Alliance (APRA), 61-62, 68, 122
Account of the Fables and Rites of the Incas, An (Molinda), 28
Ancash (department), 109
anchovies, 25
Ancón, Treaty of (1883), 60, 122
Andean foothills, 12
Andean Indians, 105
Andean Pact Common Market, 96, 112
Andes mountains, 7, 8-9, 11, 12-13, **13**, 14, 17, 18, 92, 97, **113**
animals, **5**, 17, 25, 34, **34**, 35, 43, 46, 103, 104, 117, 118
anthem, 116
Antisuyu, 30
Apurímac (department), 109
Apurímac River, 41
archaeological heritage, 7-8, 25, 97-100, **100**, 120
Archbishop's Palace, 105
area, 11, 118
Arequipa, 82, 86, 107-108, **108**, 117
Arequipa (department), 109
Argentina, 11, 41, 63, 119
Arguedas, José María, 84, 123
Arica, 122
artisans, 77-78
arts and crafts, 10, 16, **17**, 18, **18**, 20-21, **21**, 38-39, **39**, **40**, 41, **42**, 50, 51, 84, 99, 120

Atacama desert, 59, 118, 122
Atahualpa, 42, **42**, 44-47, **45**, 99, 123
Atlantic Ocean, 15, 93
Ayacucho, 122
Ayacucho, Battle of, 57, **57**, 121
Ayacucho (department), 109
Ayacucho, 90
Aymara Indians, 13, 103
Aymara language, 18, 72, 78, 116
ayulla, 35, 36, 73-75
Balboa, Vasco Núñez de, 43, **44**
Balta, Juan, 59, 123
baseball, 87
basketball, 87, 120
Bautista, Ana, 78
beaches, 107
Belaúnde Terry, Fernando, 62-64, **63**, 68, 122, 123
Belgrano, Manuel, 55-56
Belli, Carlos Herman, 84, 123
Bingham, Hiram, 100, 123
birds, 117
Blas, Camilo, 84, 123
Bolívar, Simón, 9, 57, **57**, 58, 121, 123
Bolivia, 11, 13, 48, 58, 60, 103, 117, 122
Bonaparte, Joseph, 55
Bonaparte, Napoleon, 55
borders, 11, 13
Brazil, 11, 119
bronze, 21
bullfights, 87, **87**, 120
cactus, **12**
Cajamarca (city), 44-45
Cajamarca (department), 109
Cajamarquilla, **8**
Calendaria, Feast of, 86
Callao (city), 83, 107, 117, 118
Callao (province), 109, 116
Calvo, César, 84, 123
Cambio 90, 112, 122
Camisea natural gas field, 96
Capac Yupanqui, 30, 123
capital. *See* Lima
Cardal, 98
Caribbean Sea, 13
Carlos V (Spain), 108
Castilla, Ramón, 58-59, 121, 123
Castillo, Teofilo, 84, 123

Catholic University, **80**
caudillos, 58
Cerro Baul, 20
Cerro de Pasco Corporation, 61, 66
Chachapoya, 24
Chamber of Deputies, 109, 116
Chancas, 30-31, 121
Chan-Chan, 23, **23**, 120
Change 90, 112
Charles I (Spain), 43, 47
Charles IV (Spain), 55
Chasquis, 35
Chavez, Jorge, 123
Chavins, 18, 121
Chicama Valley, 20-21
Chiclayo, 117
children, **4**, **72**
Chile, 11, 33, 41, 58, 59, 60, 113, 122
chili peppers, 53
Chimbote, 117
Chimú Empire, 23, **23**
China, 119
Chinchasuyu, 30, 32
Chincheros, **13**
Chocano, Santos, 123
Cieza de León, Pedro de, 28, 32, 33, 123
cinchona, 92
climate, 15, 68, 117, 122
clothes, 39, **74**
coal, 10
coastline, 13, 117
coat of arms, 116
Cobo, Bernabe, 123
coca, 69, **69**, 110, **110**, 118
cocaine, 69, 110, 118
cockfights, 87, 120
Codesido, Julia, 84
Collasuyu, 30
College of San Pablo, 76, 77
Colombia, 11, 33, 43, 47, 57, 58, 119
communication, 34-35, **35**, 37, 52, 59, 83, 118-119
conquistadors, 8-9, 10, 28, 52
Conservatory of Music, 85
constitution, 67, 70, 73-74, 80, 121, 122
Contisuyu, 30
copper, 10, 21, 94, 118

Cordoncanqui, José Gabriel, 54
corn, 37, **88**, 89, 90, **90**, 118
Corpus Christi, Feast of, 86
costa, 11-12, **12**
Council of Ministers, 109
courts, 109, 116
criollos, 54
Cuellar, Javier Pérez de, 123
culture, 120
Cuzco, **6**, 7, **8**, 24, **26**, 27, 30, 31-32, **32**, 33, 47, **50**, 77, 82, 86, 90, 100, 102-103, **102**, 120, 121
Cuzco (department), 109
dance competitions, 85-86
dancing, 120
departments, 11, 109, 116
de Soto, Hernando, 44-45, 46
disease. *See* health care
drugs, 69, 110, **110**, 118
earthquakes, 12, 120, 122
economy, 36, 60, 61, 63, 67, 68, 69-70, 89-96, 111, 112, 118-119, 122
Ecuador, 11, 41, 47, 57, 58, 113, 119
education, **4**, 9, 50, 59, 66, 75-77, **76**, 79-80, **79**, **80**, 90, 116, 119, 121
elections, 61-62, 70, 112, 116, 122
elevation, 117
El Mercurio Peruano, 83, 119
El Misti, 107
El Niño, 15, 68, 93, 117, 118, 122
El Paraiso, 25
encomienda, 48, 49, 72
ethnic composition, 71-72, 116
European Community, 96
everyday life, 119-120
family, 35, 75, 120
farming, 8, **8**, 9, 12, 17, 18, 20-21, **20**, 24-25, 37-38, 51-52, 52-53, **53**, 65-66, 69, **69**, 72-73, 74, **88**, 89-92, **90**, **91**, 103, 108, 110, 117, 118
Feast of Corpus Christi, 86
Federation of the Andes, 58
Ferdinand VII (Spain), 55
feria, 85-86
Festidanza, 86
festivals, 29, **29**, 85-86, **86**, 120
fishing, 24, 25, 66, 68, 93-94, **94**, 117, 118, 122

flag, 116
foods, 37-38, 120
foreign debt, 69-70, 95
foreign investments, 61, 66, 67, 96
forests, 14, 92-93, **93**, 117
France, 89
Fujimori, Alberto, 70, **70**, 95, 110, 112, 113, 122, 123
García Pérez, Alan, 68, **68**, 69, 123
Garrido Lecca, Celso, 85, 123
geography, 11-15, 117
Germany, 119
gold, 10, 28, 41, 46, 48, 49, 50, 94, 118
government, 35-36, 109, 116, 122
Government Palace, **64**
Gran Pajaten (city), 17, 122
Gran Vilaya, 23-24
Great Britain, 89, 119
Great Wall of Peru, 23
guanacos, 25
guano, 21, 59, 60, 118
guano islands, 15, 59, 121-122
Guayaquil, Ecuador, 57
Guzmán Reynoso, Abimael, 64, 122, 123
gymnastics, 120
gypsum, 10
hacienda, 72-73
health care, 42, 48, 81, **81**, 122, 119
herding, 25
Heyerdahl, Thor, 98
Historia del Nuevo Mundo (History of the New World) (Cobo), 78
history, 16-70, 120-123
holidays, 119
horse races, 87, 120
House of Poetry, 84
House of the Chosen Women, 102
housing, 105, 120
Huallaga River, 117
Huancavelica (department), 109
Huancayo, 90
Huánuco (department), 109
Huáscar, 42, **42**, 47, 124
Huayna Capac, 41, 42, 121, 124
Humboldt Current, 15, 117

hydroelectricity, 118
Ica (department), 109
Ichimay culture, 98
Illescas, Juan de, 78
Inca, 7, 8, 20, 24, 25, **26**, 27-39, **29**, **31**, **32**, **33**, **35**, **38**, **39**, **40**, 41-42, **42**, 52, 100, 121
Inca sun calendar, **38**
Inca sun festival, 86
Inca trail, **113**
independence, 9, 56, 57, 77, 121
Indians, **5**, 7-8, 9, 14, 51-52, 59, 66, 71, **113**, 116
industry, 61, 95, 118-119
Intelsat, 112
International Monetary Fund (IMF), 67, 95, 112
International Petroleum Company, 61, 63, 66, 122
Inti Raymi festival, 29, **29**, 86, **86**
Iquitos, 84, 104, **104**
iron, 10, 94, 118
irrigation, 12, 20, 98
Isla del Sol, 103
Isthmus of Panama, 43
Iturriag, Enrique, 85
Japan, 119
Junín (department), 109
kaniwa, 92, 118
Kennedy, John F., **62**
kiwicha, 91-92, 118
La Compañía Church, **102**
lakes, 13, 117
Lake Titicaca, 13, **13**, 19, 27, 32, 37, 86, 103, **103**, 117, 120, 121
La Libertad (department), 109
Lambayeque (department), 109
la montaña, 13-14
languages, 7, 18, 25, 37, 75-76, 83, 116, 119, 121
Latin American Economic System, 112
lead, 10, 118
legislative branch, 109
Leguía, Augusto B., 61, 124
life expectancy, 119
Lima, 7, 9, 47, 50, 60, 75, 77, 87, 95, 105-107, **105**, **106**, 116, 117, 118, 121
Lima (department), 109
lima beans, 53
Lima culture, 98

literature, 28-29, 59, 78-79, 84
livestock, 118
llamas, **5**, 25, 34, **34**, 35, 43, 46, 118
lomas, 25
Loreto (department), 109
lost cities of the Andes, 99
Lurin Valley, 98
Machu Picchu, 82, 100, **100**, 120
Madre de Dios (department), 109
Mama Ocllo, 27, 28, 103, 124
Manco Capac, 27, 28-29, 103, 124
maps
    political, **115**
    regional, **1**
    topographical, **2**
Mar, José de la, 58, 124
Marañó River, 32, 41, 117
market, **108**
mathematics, 35, **35**
measures, 116
Medoro, Angelino, 78
mercury, 118
mestizos, 51, 71, 73, 116
metalworking, 18
Mexico, 52
middle class, 51
military coup, 61-62, 63-64, 122
mining, 7, **10**, 48, 66, 94-95, 118
Mississippi River, 44
Moche culture, 98
Moche Valley, 20, 108
Mochicas, 21, **21**
Molinda, Cristóbal de, 28
money, 116
Moquegua, 20
Moquegua (department), 109
Morales Bermúdez, Francisco, 67-68, **67**, 124
Morón, Pedro Pablo, 78
MRTA, 111
Mt. Huascarán, 117
Museo del Oro (Gold Museum), 106
Museum of Anthropology and Archaeology, 106, 120
museums, 106, 120
music, 85, **85**, 120
name, 116
National Geographic Society, 97
National Institute of Culture, 97

National Justice Council, 109
National School of Folkloric Music and Dance, 85
National School of Theater Arts, 84
National Stadium at Lima, 120
National Symphony Orchestra, 85
National Theater Company, 84
National University of Huamanga, 64
natural gas, 10, 96, 118
natural resources, 10, **10**, 14, 21, 41, 59-60
Nazca, **17**, 22-23, **22**
Nazca River, 22
New Laws, 49, 121
newspapers, 83, 84, 119
nitrate, 59-60, 122
Non-aligned Movement, 112
North Peru, 58
Núñez de Balboa, Vasco, 43, **44**
offshore islands. *See* guano islands
oil, 10, 14, 96, 118, 122
Ollantaytambo, 120
Olympic Games, 87
Organization of American States, 112
Pachacamac, 98-99, 120
Pachacuti, 31-32, 41, 124
Pacific Ocean, 7, 11, 13, 15
Palace of the President, 63
Palma, Ricardo, 84, 124
Panama, 57, 58
Pan-American Highway, 82, **82**, 98, 118
Paracas, 99
Pardo, Manuel, 59
Pasco (department), 61, 109
Peralta y Barnuevo, Don Pedro de, 78-79, 124
Pérez de Alecio, Mateo, 78, 124
Peru Current, 15, 117
Peruvian-Bolivian Confederation, 58
Peruvian desert, 11-12, **12**
petroleum, 10, 14, 96, 118, 122
Philip, King (Spain), 75
phosphate, 10
Pisac, **20**
Piura (city), 117
Piura (department), 109

Pizarro, Francisco, 8, 28, 43-47, **44**, **45**, 47, 105, 121, 124
Pizarro, Hernando, 45, 46, 99
Plaza de Armas, 63, 103, 105, 108, 120
Plaza de San Martín, 105
Plaza Huacaypata, 103
population, 105, 117
ports, 12, 83, **83**, 107, 118
potatoes, 37, 53, **53**, **88**, 89, 90, 118
Potosi, 48
poverty, 7, 9
Prado, Manuel, 61-62, **62**
Pre-Inca Indians, 16-25, **17**, **18**, **19**, **20**, **21**, **22**, **23**, **24**, 120-121
president, 109, 116
Presidential Palace, 105, 120
prime minister, 109
Puno (city), 82, 86, 90, 103, **103**
Puno (department), 109
Quechua Indians, 13, 30, 103
Quechua language, 7, 37, 75-76, 77, 78, 116, 119, 121
Quillabamba, 82
quince, 90-91, **91**, 118
quipus, 35, **35**, 36
Quito, Ecuador, 41, 42
radio, 83, 118-119
railroads, 59, 60, 82, **83**, 118
rain forests, 11, 13, 14, 74, 117
record keeping, 36-37, **36**
regions, 11-14
religion, 49-50, **50**, 80-81, 106-107, 116
rest houses (*tambos*), 34
revolutionary government, 64-65
Revolutionary Government of the Armed Forces, 64
Rimac River, 105
Río Moquegua, 20
rivers, 12, 117
roads, 33-34, **33**, **34**, 37, 59, 82, **82**, 118
Roca Rey, Joaquin, 84
Rodriguez, Elvira, 78
Roman Catholic church, 50, **50**, 75, 76-77, 80-81, 116
Romualdo, Alejandro, 84
Rosa, Luisa de, 78
Saavedra, Luis de, 75
Sabogal, José, 84, 124

Sacsahuamán, **38**, 102
Salazar Bondy, Sebastian, 84, 124
sand dunes, 12
San Martín, José de, 9, 56, **56**, 57, **57**, 121, 124
San Martin (department), 109
San Miguel de Piura, 44, 121
Santa Cruz, Andrés, 58
Santo Domingo, monastery of, **24**
Santo Domingo Church, 103
Santo Tomas, Fray Domingo de, 75, 76, 121, 124
selva, 13-14, 74, 92, **93**, 104, 117
Senate, 109, 116
Shining Path, 64, **64**, 69, 93, 110-112, **111**, 122, 123
sierra, 12-13, 79
silver, 10, 41, 46, 48, 49, 94, 118
Sipan, 98
slavery, 59
Smithsonian Institution, 97
soccer, 87, 120, 122
social classes, 49-50, 51-52, 60-61, 71-72
social system, 71-72
social welfare, 120
Southern Hemisphere, 15
Southern Railway, 82, **82**
South Peru, 58
Soviet Union, 94, 95, 112-113
Spanish conquest/rule, 8-9, 28, 43-54, **44**, **45**, **46**, **47**, 90, 119, 121
sports and recreation, 87, **87**, 120, 122
squatters, 72, **72**, **73**, 105, **106**, 111, 120
standard of living, 66
Standard Oil Company of New Jersey (Exxon), 61

stonework, **18**
street vendors, **106**
Sucre, Antonio José de, 9, 121, 124
sugarcane, 90, 118
Sun Gate, 19, **19**
Sun Temple, 99
suspension bridges, 34, **34**
Swayne, Enrique Solari, 84, 124
Szyszlo, Fernando de, 84
Tacna (department), 109
Tacna (province), 60, 122
Tahuantinsuyu, 30
Tambopata Wildlife Preserve, 104, 117
Tampu Machay, 102
television, 83, 118-119
Tello, Julio C., 99
Temple of the Sun, 21, 46, 50, 103
terrorism, 69, 96, 110-112, 122, 123
Tiahuanaco Empire, 19, **19**, 120, 121
tin, 21
Toledo, Francisco de, 49, 73, 77
tomatoes, 53
Torre, Victor Raul Haya de la, 124
trade, 59, 90, 91, 93, 94, 96, 104, 119
Trans-Andean Highway, 104
transportation, 12, 33-34, **33**, **34**, 37, 59, 60, 82-83, **82**, **83**, 104, 107-108, **107**, 118
Trujillo, 56, 61, 86, 108, 117, 121, 122
Tucume, 98
Tumbes (city), 43
Tumbes (department), 109
Tupa Inca, 41, 124
Tupac Amaru, 54, 124

Tupac Amaru II, 54, 124
Tupac Amaru Revolutionary Movement (MRTA), 111
Ucayali (department), 109
Ucayali River, 83, 117
unemployment, 112
United Army of Liberation, 57
United Nations, 112
United States, 66, 69, 89, 119
United States Drug Enforcement Administration, 110
University of San Marcos, 50, 61, 76-77, **76**, 119, 121
Upper Huallaga Valley, 69, **69**, 110
Upper Peru, 56, 58
Urcon, 31
Urubamba River, 100
Valasco Alvarado, Juan, **65**, 124
Valcarel, Juan, 85
Vallejois, Cesar, 84, 124
vanadium, 118
Vargas Llosa, Mario, 84, 124
Vega, Garcilasa de la, 28
vegetation, **12**, 14, **14**, 117
Velasco Alvarado, Juan, 64-65, 66, 67
Venezuela, 57, 58, 119, 121
Viracocha, 30, 124
volleyball, 120
War of the Pacific, 59-60, 122
weights, 116
whales, 25
women, 122
World Wildlife Fund (WWF), 92-93
Yanesha Forestry Cooperative, 92-93
Yanesha Indians, 92, 93
Yupanqui, 31, **31**, 124
Zavaleta, Carlos, 84
zinc, 10, 94, 118

About the Author

Emilie Utteg Lepthien earned a BS and MA degree and a Certificate in School Administration from Northwestern University. She taught third grade, upper-grade science and social studies, and was principal of Wicker Park School in Chicago.

Mrs. Lepthien has written and narrated science and social studies scripts for WBEZ of the Chicago Board of Education. She has been a co-author of primary social studies books for Rand McNally and Company and has served as educational consultant for Encyclopaedia Britannica Films. She is the author of *Ecuador, Iceland, Greenland, Australia,* and *The Philippines* in the Enchantment of the World series. She has traveled to all seven continents and is interested in photography as well as writing.